.N

BOMBER

COMMAND

The Air Ministry Account
of Bomber Command's
Offensive Against the Axis

September, 1939—July, 1941

LONDON: HIS MAJESTY'S STATIONERY OFFICE

BLENHE

List of Contents

To be purchased from His Majesty's Stationery Office at : York House, Kingsway, London, W.C.2 ; 120, George St., Edinburgh, 2 ; 39-41, King St., Manchester, 2 ; 1, St. Andrew's Crescent, Cardiff ; 80, Chichester St., Belfast ; or through any bookseller
Price 1/6 net or 20/- for 15 copies.   S.O. Code No. 70/380

WHITLEY

ISSUED FOR THE AIR MINISTRY BY THE MINISTRY OF INFORMATION
CROWN COPYRIGHT RESERVED. FIRST PUBLISHED 1941
COVER PRINTED BY HARRISON & SONS LTD., LONDON ; TEXT BY THOMAS NELSON & SONS LTD., EDINBURGH

The first target. The "Admiral Scheer," taken by surprise, seen through rain squalls from the Blenheim which skimmed the tender at her stern and bombed her.

BOMBER COMMAND

I—War Telegram

SOME TEN MINUTES before eleven o'clock on the morning of Sunday, 3rd September, 1939, a number of high officers and civil servants had gathered together in a room in Richmond Terrace, Whitehall. On a table, ready to be consulted, was a copy of the Government War Book, in which is set out the necessary action to be taken on the outbreak of hostilities by the Royal Navy, the Army and the Royal Air Force and by all Departments of State. The men in that room did not consult this book, for they were already well instructed in the directions it contained. Many of them had helped to revise these during the months separating that warm September morning from the blustering March day—the 15th of the month—on which the German armoured divisions entered Prague. The precautionary measures had all been taken. Reservists of the three Services had joined their posts or were hastening to them. The flying squadrons of the Auxiliary Air Force had been put on a war footing. The Observer Corps manned their posts; the A.R.P. Services were ready. The men assembled in that room did not talk much. They were awaiting a message from Berlin. Few, if any, of them doubted what it would be.

The message arrived. It was from the British Ambassador to the German Reich and its purport was that there was no message. Hitler had not replied to the ultimatum of the British Government. While they were talking of this, the Secretary to the Cabinet entered. "Gentlemen," he said, "we are at war with Germany. The Prime Minister directs that the 'War Telegram' be despatched immediately." The hour was a few minutes after eleven. In the streets outside men and women watched the barrage balloons rise to operational height. At 11.15, the Prime Minister began to speak to this country and to the world. While he was still at the microphone the War Telegram went out to all those in authority appointed to receive it. Relayed through Group Headquarters, it reached the Commander of the Royal Air Force Station at Wyton. Upon the aerodrome, waiting to take off, was a Blenheim of Bomber Command. Three men were standing by—the pilot, the observer who was a naval officer, and an air gunner. They had been waiting since the 1st September, the day on which the Germans launched their attack on Poland. A minute after noon, about half an hour after the War Telegram had been received, the Blenheim was airborne. Some two hours later its crew were busy photographing units of the German Fleet, then on its way out of Wilhelmshaven. The Blenheim was flying at 24,000 feet. At that height in the conditions of weather then prevailing the wireless set froze, so that it was not until 4.50 in the afternoon, when the aircraft returned, that Bomber Command and the Admiralty became aware of the position of the war's first target. That evening an entry appeared in the log-book of the squadron: "Duty successful. 75 photos taken of German Fleet. The first R.A.F. aircraft to cross the German frontier."

On the next day as the result of a second reconnaissance the German cruiser "Leipzig" was discovered near the entrance to

Wilhelmshaven, four destroyers in the Jade Bay and two warships at Brunsbüttel at the western end of the Kiel Canal. Twenty-nine Blenheims and Wellingtons took off in the afternoon to attack these units of the German Fleet. The weather was very bad. There was heavy rain and low cloud over all that part of the coasts of Germany. Though many of our aircraft went astray, one reached Brunsbüttel and bombed a warship with no observed result. Five Blenheims reached the Schillig Roads. They were carrying 500-lb. bombs, fused for a delay of eleven seconds. Up the Roads they flew in open formation some 500 feet above the sea. Two of them in the rear lost touch, but the other three held on and presently sighted, between rain squalls, a German battleship, the " Von Scheer." She was to port of them. No. 2 of the squadron, flying to starboard and abreast of his leader, pulled up over him, turning very sharply. This manœuvre put him in a position to attack first. He did so, but his first bomb missed the ship by ten yards and his second failed to leave the aircraft.

Meanwhile his leader was coming in to the attack. To deliver it he descended almost to the surface of the water. A tender along-side the stern of the warship provided momentary cover. The leader skimmed over this and pulled up just high enough to clear the mast of the " Von Scheer." His observer saw men leaning against the rails of the ship and a line of washing hanging out to dry. Then the bombs fell and pieces from the catapult gear, used to launch the ship's aircraft, flew into the air. The third Blenheim attacked a second later, but its crew were uncertain whether they had scored hits. The attack was a complete surprise. One moment the German crew were taking their ease on deck, the next they were doubling to their action stations as the British bombers climbed up and away into the thick air, bullets flashing past their wings " like small blue electric sparks."

These Blenheims were followed by five more, who attacked from a very low level. Only one returned. The exact fate of the others is not known, but months later a German, talking of this raid to a friend in a compartment of a train crossing Northern Italy, remarked upon the reckless gallantry of their crews. It appeared that the crew of at least one Blenheim attacked the enemy so closely that the blast of their bombs when they exploded on the warship destroyed their aircraft. Our total losses were two Wellingtons and five Blenheims.

With this attack the war began. In skill, resource and resolution, it was typical of all which were to follow, and showed clearly to those in command of the Royal Air Force—though they had never doubted that it was so—that the men whose fathers had fought the Germans in the last war were in every way worthy of their begetters.

The first record. A facsimile of the first operations record of the war—a reconnaissance flight over Wilhelmshaven.

(*24c5—226) WL 26310=1577 14,000 12/36 T.S. 667

Appendix *Appendix H*   R.A.F. For

OPERATIONS RECORD BOOK.

DETAIL OF WORK CARRIED OUT.

From 1200 hrs. 3 / 9 / 39 to 2359 hrs. 3 / 9 / 39   By 139 Sqdn.   No. of pages used for day

Aircraft Type and No.	Crew.	Duty.	Time Up.	Time Down.	Remarks.	Reference
Blenheim MK. IV N6215	F/O McPherson. Cdr. Thompson. c/c. Arrowsmith.	Photo Reco.	1200.	1650.	Duty successful. 75 photos taken of GERMAN fleet. The first Royal Air Force aircraft to cross the GERMAN frontier.	

Captain and crew form a team, upon whose close co-ordination the success of every flight depends : (left to right) navigator, radio operator, rear gunner, captain, second pilot.

II—Captains and Crews

THIS RECORD is, for the most part, the story of the Battles, the Blenheims and the Hampdens, the Wellingtons and the Whitleys. Our larger and more modern aircraft, the Stirlings, the Manchesters, the Halifaxes, the Flying Fortresses and the rest, enter it only at the end. It has been the aircraft constructed before the war that have up

till now been the chief instruments of the attack on Germany. In these aircraft the men of Bomber Command have flown some twenty-four million miles during the period under review. It was a period of preparation for events on the threshold of which we are now standing. Unlike the Luftwaffe, which, from the beginning, was provided with large numbers of bombers, the Royal Air Force was, on the 3rd September, 1939, stronger in fighters. That the policy of giving priority to the creation and training of a strong fighter force was right, no one who saw or who remembers the Battle of Britain, fought and won over the Southern Counties of England during the

Pilot and second pilot—" Brave yet cautious, cool yet daring."

one of a team and that that team is not flying separated from him in another Hurricane or Spitfire, but in the same aircraft, crouched over the navigator's table or hunched up in the gun turrets. He must be imaginative, yet not be dismayed by his own imagination, brave yet cautious, cool yet daring.

The men of Bomber Command are appointed to fulfil a special mission. Their life is not that of other men—not that even of those in the other branches of the service. Its very physical conditions are different. For them nowadays much of the night is the day, much of the day a time for sleep and repose. Discipline is constant yet flexible and its effect is to cause these men

Navigator. The key man in a bomber aircraft.

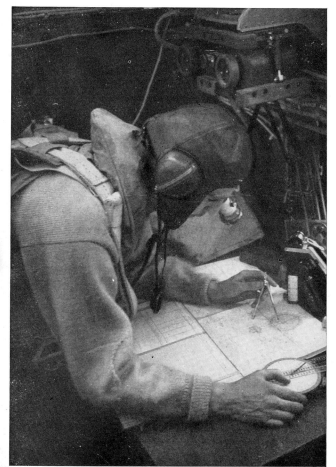

to display an informed capacity to meet life as a familiar, sometimes an exacting, but always a common, friend. Triumph and disaster are met and vanquished together. If the first be their lot, the thankfulness, the exaltation are shared equally by all the crew; if the second, if " the whirligig of time brings in its revenges," they have mounted it together and together they have ridden it to the end. It is this ability to be at once absorbed but not blinded by responsibilities in which all have a vital part, that makes it natural for a sergeant to be the captain of an aircraft in which the rear gunner is an officer or for a group captain to fly as second pilot to a flight lieutenant. Anyone who has watched a crew discussing their route to the target or boarding their bomber before the take-off or facing the intelligence officer at the journey's end, knows this to be true.

When they are not required to take part in the night's operations they occupy themselves during the day with training, with the care of their equipment and guns, with the testing of their aircraft and with station duties. After a sortie they pass their time in various ways. Much of it is spent in sleep either in their own quarters in the station itself or in dormitories fitted up elsewhere, the object being to secure for them as large a measure of quiet as possible. In some places they are to be found in small modern houses, each of which holds all or part of a crew; in others fifty or sixty men may sleep in the panelled rooms of a manor house already old when Hampden defied King Charles, Marlborough won Blenheim and Wellington cast down the French.

In their waking hours they play games, read, occupy their leisure in whatever way best pleases them. Two things are noticeable. There is no tabu on talking " shop " in the Mess and the wireless is rarely silent. Is this, perhaps, because the noise of engines is so much a part of their lives that silence

summer and autumn of 1940, will wish to deny. Had fighters and fighter pilots then been lacking, defeat and disaster would have been inevitable.

The bomber force, however, though in numbers far from equal to that of the enemy, was compact, ready and resolute. Its task was to attack the enemy according to plan. It had been trained to carry out raids in daylight as well as by night, and it had been provided with aircraft which it was hoped would be sufficient for that purpose, both in respect of bomb load and armament. The training had not been carried out without difficulty, for in the spring and summer of 1939 the Wellingtons, Whitleys and Hampdens were still new and comparatively untried aircraft. Before their appearance on the scene the men of Bomber Command had been flying far less powerful aircraft such as the Handley-Page Harrow, the Hawker Hind, and the Vickers Wellesley. These carried a crew of two or, at the most, three, which meant that most of the responsibility during flight fell upon the shoulders of the pilot. With the bigger aircraft, however, carrying crews of four, five, and six, the necessity for closer team work soon became apparent. A further stage in flying training known as operational training was therefore introduced. "Captains and Crews" is a phrase constantly recurring in reports on operations. It is of importance, and its significance must be clearly understood. It means exactly what it says. A bomber, unlike a fighter, is flown not only by the pilot but also by the air observer, the wireless operator and the air gunner. They form a team and the success or failure of the flight depends on the closest and most intimate co-operation of all on board. The captain and his second pilot do the actual flying; the observer navigates and drops the bombs; the wireless operator helps the navigator and with the air gunner does the fighting. The same spirit and practice of co-ordination is required of a bomber crew as of the crew of a racing eight or the members of a football eleven. To rewrite the old saying, their motto is, and must be, " United we fly, divided we fall." This lesson has been learnt by the men of Bomber Command from the very beginning. More than anything else it is the secret of their success.

The bomber pilot differs in training and environment from his colleague flying a Spitfire or a Hurricane. A pilot of the Royal Air Force is subjected at an early stage to a process of selection by which it is determined whether he is better fitted to fly a fighter or a bomber. Both will have to fly aircraft; both will wear pilot's wings; both will be controlled, to a certain extent, by wireless from the ground or from their leader; but here their ways diverge. The fighter pilot is in action for an hour and a half to two hours at most, often far less. He is usually led into the fight by his squadron leader. Once battle is joined it is every man for himself.

The Bomber Pilot

Very different, but equally important, qualities are required of a bomber pilot. He must be capable of considerable physical and mental endurance, for it may be necessary for him to remain nine, ten, eleven, or even twelve hours in the air, and to fly for the most part of that time over hostile territory or across the unfriendly sea. During much of the flight he may find his aircraft the object of an attack by enemy fighters far faster and more heavily armed. By reason of their greater speed his assailants can break off and renew their assault at any moment. Surprise, that weapon which more than any other wins a fight, is theirs to wield at will. The bomber pilot must fly doggedly on, defending himself with the aid of darkness and cloud outside and with the skill of his crew and their machine guns inside. The bomber pilot must not forget that he is

Radio operator. He helps the navigator and, with the air gunner, does the fighting.

seems an unnatural void? They are of necessity subjected to strain. It is the inevitable accompaniment of their calling. They are men, for the most part, in the prime of youth. For them the shapes of life and death are very real. Yet any place more free from an atmosphere of strain than a bomber station would be hard to find. In writing of it, comparisons are more than usually odious, but perhaps it may be likened to that found in an inn frequented by mountaineers. Roped together, these go out to the assault of high and difficult peaks. Each

man's life may depend, at any moment, on the skill and courage of his comrades tied to the same cord. The hours they spend overcoming the obstacles of nature to reach the ultimate point of naked or snow-bound rock which marks the summit, breed in them a spirit of fellowship denied to other men. It is this spirit, refined and made keener by the fire of war and by the sense of what is at stake, that informs the men of Bomber Command.

The key man in a bomber aircraft is the navigator. His task is threefold. He must

Rear gunner. "The striking thing about a tail turret is the sense of detachment it gives you."

give his pilot the directions necessary to enable the bomber to reach the target at the right time; he must aim and release the bombs and he must bring the aircraft and its crew safely back to base. Under ideal conditions his task is not difficult; but conditions are rarely ideal. Darkness, clouds, air currents, all singly or together, are his foes. His main preoccupation is with air currents, for he finds himself, unless the wind is directly ahead or astern, in much the same predicament as a man trying to swim straight across a river disregarding the force of the current. It cannot be done. The speed and direction of the wind have to be calculated and taken into constant consideration throughout the flight.

The navigator has certain aids to help him in his calculations and enable him to check his position. These are: radio position finding, usually known as " radio fix," map reading and astronomical navigation. The first is limited by distance ; the second is useless unless landmarks can be seen ; the third can be used only when the stars are visible. The skilful navigator makes judicious use of all three. He is usually working in conditions opposed to accurate calculations, for he carries out his duties in a cramped space, wearing bulky clothes and an oxygen mask. Yet the proportion of bombers that reach their objectives, always very high, is growing higher. The target is hit again and again. Nearly two years of flying under war conditions have taught invaluable lessons the results of which are each night becoming more apparent. " The wind and waves are always on the side of the ablest navigator " runs a quotation from Gibbon upon the wall of the briefing-room of one bomber squadron. In the past many of the greatest sea navigators were British. To-day our air navigators are showing themselves to be worthy of their forbears.

Their other task is to aim the aircraft and drop the bombs from it. To hit a target is not easy. There is no barrel to direct the bomb as the rifle barrel directs the bullet. Bombs are not " projected "—that is thrown --but " released "—that is dropped. Moreover, they fall from something which is not stationary, but moving at a high speed. The bomb at the start, therefore, has the same speed and direction as the aircraft. Air resistance acts as a brake, but its effect is not great. The bomb does not fall vertically but moves forward as well as downward in a curved path. For example, if a bomber is flying at 10,000 feet at a speed of 200 m.p.h., a 500-lb. bomb will strike the ground more than $1\frac{1}{4}$ miles ahead of the point where it was released. But enemy defences are probably active. There are searchlights and flak. The bomb-aimer has no time for higher mathematics. He uses a bomb-sight on which he has set height, air-speed, size of bomb and other factors. This instrument automatically gives a correct aim. At the right moment the bomb is released and travels steadily towards the target.

The wind has little effect on the flight of the bomb once it has left the aircraft, but an important influence which affects bombing is the strength and direction of the wind in which the aircraft itself is flying. This must be exactly calculated and set on the bomb-sight. To attack a small target, for example a narrow bridge, the bomb-aimer will release a " stick " of bombs, that is, a number in succession designed to straddle the target. The chances that one of the bombs will hit it are thereby increased. Up to a point, the greater the height from which it is released, the greater are the striking velocity and penetrating power of a bomb. The importance of this factor will be seen during the course of this narrative in relation to our attacks on enemy shipping. Armour-piercing bombs aimed, for example, at the " Scharnhorst," " Gneisenau " or " Prinz Eugen," have to be dropped from a considerable height if they are to go through their protected decks.

Ice, Fog, Storms, Fire

It has already been said that one of the main obstacles besetting a navigator in the fulfilment of his task is the weather. Apart from violent changes in the speed and force of air currents, electrical storms, fog and the formation of ice on an aircraft in flight are formidable adversaries. Electrical storms may cause the aircraft to become in effect an electrical conductor. This means a danger of fire in those parts of it through which the electrical discharge cannot easily pass. Apart from the risk of fire, the navigational instruments, particularly the compass, may become unserviceable. In a storm this can be very serious ; for if the pilot cannot see the land he is completely dependent on such artificial aids to navigation.

THE FIRST SCENE OF BATTLE

The main targets of Bomber Command, during the first eight months of war, were Germany's fleet and seaplane bases in the North Sea and the enemy-occupied ports and airfields of Norway.

N

ATLANTIC

OCEAN

ORKNEY IS
HOY
SCAPA FLOW

ABERDEEN

DUNDEE

EDINBURGH
GLASGOW
BERWICK

DUMFRIES
NEWCASTLE
CARLISLE
MIDDLESBRO'

LONDONDERRY
NORTHERN IRELAND
BELFAST

YORKSHIRE

GALWAY
PRESTON
HULL
LIVERPOOL
MANCHESTER
CHESTER
DUBLIN

LINCOLNSHIRE

DERBY NOTTINGHAM

WATERFORD WEXFORD
BIRMINGHAM
WYTON
QUEENSTOWN
OXFORD

EAST A

CARDIFF
LONDON
BRISTOL

SOUTHAMPTON
PORTSMOUTH
WEYMOUTH

PLYMOUTH

ENGLISH CHANNEL

CHERBOURG
DIEPPE
LE HAVRE

STATUTE MILES

0 10 20 30 40 50   100

SHETLAND IS TO BERGEN 227 MILES.

BERGEN

N O R W A Y

FORNEBU
OSLO

DRAMMEN
FJORD

OSLO FJORD

STAVANGER

KRISTIANSAND

SKAGER RAK

GOTHENBURG

COAST TO STAVANGER 410 MILES.

NORTH SEA

AALBORG

D E N M A R K

THE SOUND

BALTIC
SEA

HORN'S REEF

GREAT BELT

COPENHAGEN

MALMÖ

LITTLE BELT

BORNHOLM

SYLT

ECKERNFÖRDE

"HORNETS' NEST"

KIEL

HELIGOLAND

WARNEMÜNDE

LINCOLNSHIRE COAST TO KIEL 410 MILES.

WANGEROOG

KIEL CANAL

R. ELBE

NORDERNEY

SCHILLIG ROAD

CUXHAVEN

BRUNSBÜTTEL

LÜBECK

POLITZ

BORKUM

WILHELMSHAVEN

JADE

BREMERHAVEN

STETTIN

DELFZIL

EMDEN

R. ELBE

GRONINGEN

OLDENBURG

HAMBURG

YARMOUTH

R. EMS

BREMEN

WITTENBURG

H O L L A N D

VECHT

YMUIDEN

AMSTERDAM

WESER R.

HANOVER

R. ODER

BERLIN

WICH

THE HAGUE
HOOK OF HOLLAND

ROTTERDAM

G E R M A N Y

MAGDEBURG

GATE

R. MAAS

HAMM

RUHR

LEIPZIG

FLUSHING

DUISBURG

DRESDEN

DUNKIRK

ANTWERP

DÜSSELDORF

R. SCHELDT

COLOGNE

LILLE

BRUSSELS

LIEGE

B E L G I U M

ORE MOUNTAINS

R. RHINE

LUXEMBURG

COBLENZ

FRANKFURT

PRAGUE

R. MOLDAU

R. OISE

R. MEUSE

R. MAIN

R. RHINE

NS

F R A N C E

Ice may be formed on an aircraft when flying through certain types of cloud, particularly cumulus. Condensation will occur on the wings and a sudden drop in temperature causes the water thus formed to freeze. Ice on the wings may deprive them of their lift. Ice in the carburettor of the engine may choke out its life.

The Aircraft They Flew

BATTLE

Finally, a word as to the aircraft flown by the men of Bomber Command.

Nine types of bomber aircraft have been used in Europe by Bomber Command during the period covered by this narrative. They are the Fairey Battle, the Bristol Blenheim, the Vickers-Armstrong Wellington, the Armstrong-Whitworth Whitley, the Handley-Page Hampden, the Short Stirling, the Avro Manchester, the Handley-Page Halifax and the American Boeing Flying Fortress. The Battle has not been used by the Bomber Command in bombing operations since October, 1940. The Stirling, Manchester, Halifax and Fortress did not operate before February, 1941.

All these aircraft, with the exception of the Wellington, and, in one small respect, the Whitley, are built of metal, with stressed metal coverings. All, with the exception of the Battle, are multi-engined, mid-winged monoplanes, the single wing being placed so that half the depth of the fuselage is above the wing and half below it. The Fortress is a multi-engined low-wing monoplane. The Whitley differs in construction from the others only in the after-part of the wings, which is fabric covered. The Wellington is entirely fabric covered and is remarkable for its geodetic construction. The surface of the aircraft is made up of panels consisting of a diagonal criss-cross metal framework, like a trellis or a large-meshed net, on which the fabric covering is stretched.

An armament of machine guns is carried in all these aircraft, primarily for defence against fighters but also capable of offensive use against ground targets. In all types except the Battle and Hampden hydraulically-operated gun turrets are fitted. These turrets make it possible for the gunner to train his guns against the pressure of the air stream at high speeds. The tail turret of the Whitley mounts four Browning guns, controlled by one rear gunner sitting in the turret. This is a formidable armament to turn against pursuing fighters. If the rear gunner can hold his fire until the enemy is well within range, experience has shown that it will go hardly with the pursuer. Four types of turret are used in R.A.F. bombers; they mount variously, one, two or four guns.

A bomber will carry no more fuel than is needed to take it to the target and back, with the necessary margin for safety. The fuel and bomb loads, therefore, vary with the range of the target chosen. At the beginning of the war Bomber Command had at its disposal two main classes of bombers—the medium type, represented by the Battles and Blenheims, capable of carrying loads of between 1,000 and 1,500 lb. for a circuit of action of 1,000 miles at a long-range cruising speed, and a heavier bomber carrying either several times the bomb load for the same distance or a smaller load for a longer distance. In the latter class were the

Wellingtons, the Whitleys and the Hampdens.

Thus, from the outset of hostilities, many of the aircraft of the Bomber Command were able to fly with substantial loads to points as far as 800 miles from their bases and return—a total distance of 1,600 miles.

From our bomber aerodromes in East Anglia, Lincolnshire and Yorkshire the approximate distance to Berlin and back is 1,100 miles ; to Hamburg or Mannheim and back is 900 miles ; to Hamm and back is 800 miles ; to the Ruhr or Cologne and back is 700 miles. There were more distant objectives. To Warsaw and back is approximately

HAMPDEN

1,600 miles ; to Danzig or Vienna and back is 1,400 miles ; to Prague and back is 1,200 miles. By refuelling at bases in France near Rheims the return journeys to Warsaw and Vienna, for example, were reduced to 1,300 and 900 miles respectively.

In attacks on Northern Italy our Whitleys have flown from Yorkshire. The distance from there to Turin and back is 1,350 miles. By refuelling at an aerodrome on the south coast of England, the distance is reduced to 1,050 miles. From North-East Scotland to Oslo and back the distance is 950 miles ; to

Bergen and back, 700 miles ; to Trondheim and back, 1,200 miles. From Lincolnshire to Courtrai in Belgium, and back, a flight often made by our Blenheim bombers during the early stages of the Battle of France, is a distance of 450 miles.

Since the war began the five types then in use have been modified and improved. Four new types have been brought into service. These are the Stirling, Manchester, Halifax, and Boeing Flying Fortress. The Stirling, Halifax and Fortress are four-engined bombers. The Stirling is our largest bomber. It has a wing span of 99 feet, a length of 87 feet 3 inches, and a height of 22 feet 9 inches. Its defensive armament is very heavy. No further details of this aircraft and no details of the Halifax or Manchester can as yet be made public.

With these new aircraft at its disposal Bomber Command has a much greater striking range and, what is even more important, can deliver on the nearer targets a much heavier attack, aircraft for aircraft, bomb load for bomb load, than at the beginning of the war. It must be remembered that all the new American types are not at present in use by Bomber Command. Consolidated Liberators, Douglas Bostons and Havocs, Glenn Martin Marylands, Lockheed Hudsons, all of them American aircraft of high performance, have so far been allotted to other Commands of the Royal Air Force where they are proving their worth.

WHITLEY

BLENHEIMS

The Governments of Great Britain and France adopted as a basis of their operations the rules for aerial warfare drawn up at The Hague in 1923, even though they had never been ratified. These rules attempted to provide a definition of what does constitute a military target, which may be suitably subjected to air bombardment, and what does not. According to this definition military targets include, among others, "military forces, works, establishments or depots, factories constituting important and well-known centres engaged in the manufacture of arms, munitions or distinctively military supplies; lines of communica-tion or transportation used for military purposes."

It was, of course, realised that it would certainly be necessary, at some determined moment, to attack legitimate vital targets wherever they were situated. The rules drawn up seventeen years before at The Hague, while they did not provide an alto-gether complete or satisfactory definition of military objectives, proceeded on the generally accepted basis that in the conditions of modern warfare targets directly concerned with the prosecution of the war might legitimately be attacked. Considerations of humanity therefore could not constitute a legiti-

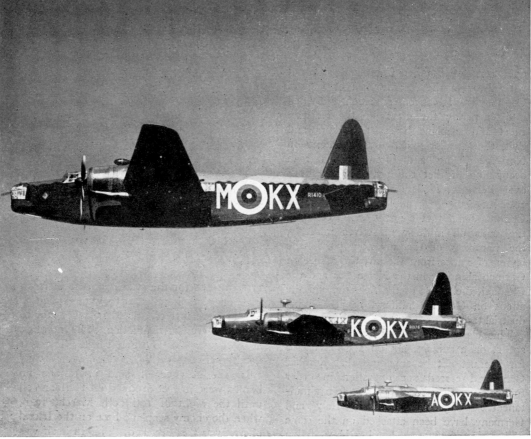

WELLINGTONS

capital ships, two sub
surface and three enem

The attack on Brunsl
Roads took place on tl
declared and was follo
reconnaissance carried
one of their objects wa:
concerning a reported c
bombers on the Ger
There proved to be n
The photographic reco
these aircraft, soon k
Blenheims, were extenc
land Bight and thei
Germany. These cons
fairly severe casualtie
navigators making thei
experience of flying lo
sea. They learnt it as
became accustomed to
all kinds of weather
guide them. The pho
back with them enable
accurate picture to be
bases, factories, roads
and other places of n

Challeng
signal to

mate reason for never attacking land targets.

Why in these circumstances the German Fleet was chosen as the first objective to be attacked rather than German industries, communications or troop concentrations is a question frequently asked. It cannot be answered fully at this moment. Future historians will doubtless do so. To answer it immediately would involve the discussion of matters of high policy and of strategy outside the scope of a record published while we are still at war.

There was one reason for using our small but efficient bombing force on sea and not on land targets. It was not the only reason,

but it was very strong and full weight was given to it by the Government. It was this.

Though not nearly so large as it was in the war of 1914-1918, the German Navy was, nevertheless, a powerful weapon. It could raid our vital seaborne trade; it could do great damage, even though it was in no position, in view of its numerical inferiority, to fight a general fleet action. If it could be attacked, disabled or even destroyed from the air, a menace would be removed. This consideration was of paramount importance to an island race, dependent for so much of its supplies and food on seaborne traffic.

This narrative is concerned only with the

operations
with those
Commands
into ten pa
Fleet and
Sylt, the "
Norway d
occupation
over Belgi
16th June,
Command
the raids
the bombi
laying of r
German sh
Channel, t
attack on
dustrial tar

This cla
speak, on
for it mus
Command
to begin a
taneous.
Germany
night. L
together.

Our kr
complete.
supplemer
war is ov
amount o
this can o
of the cre
from pho
sources.

It is, I
broad str
Bomber C
two mont
in places.
colours
throughou
shed by
durance
accomplis

week-end. It was therefore decided that Bomber Command should undertake reconnaissance in strength, using aircraft equipped with bombs and ready to attack. In pursuance of this policy, a squadron of Hampdens patrolling the Heligoland Bight on 29th September, in two formations of six and five, found and attacked two enemy destroyers. Owing to what appears to have been an error in timing, the two formations became separated, and when the second reached the area the enemy had been roused to action. The five aircraft composing this formation were intercepted. None of them returned, and the Germans claim to have shot them all down with the loss of two of their own fighters. The other formation, attacking the destroyers from 300 feet, was met with heavy pom-pom fire, and a well-aimed shell went through the nose of the leading aircraft of the first flight. It struck the pilot on the elbow causing him involuntarily to pull back the stick and swoop sharply upwards. The other two aircraft close behind followed their leader. All the bombs fell into the sea wide of their mark. The experience gained from this raid and that of 4th September appeared to show that a level attack on heavily-armed naval vessels from such a low height was likely to prove a costly undertaking. Moreover, the penetrating power of the bombs dropped is uncertain, and the risk that they may bounce off the decks or turrets very real.

At intervals throughout the autumn months the German warships made a number of sorties into the Atlantic, and on 23rd of November, during a sweep off Iceland, one of them, the " Deutschland," sank the armed cruiser H.M.S. " Rawalpindi." A striking force of bombers stood by at Scottish bases from 24th November to 2nd December in the vain hope that the weather would allow them to attack her.

So much for attacks at sea. When enemy vessels were close to their bases the problem became more complicated. At a well-defended base such as Wilhelmshaven, German fighters, it was observed, took the air within ten minutes of the sighting of the objective by our bombers. They were able to do so because of the warning they received from a line of " flak " ships some seventy miles west of Heligoland. It was, indeed, obvious that strong defence forces were stationed in all these German North Sea bases. The Bight soon came to be known as " The Hornets' Nest." Was it possible to attack warships when they were close to such defences ? It should be remembered that at this stage British policy was to give the bombers means of self-protection and to rely on this and on the collective fire of a bomber formation to beat off fighter attack. Our bomber force had been primarily designed and intended for use as a day force for attacks on land targets. Certain considerations had caused it to be used only against ships which had not as yet been heavily defended by fighter aircraft. If the enemy's ships were to be attacked suddenly without previous reconnaissance so as to ensure surprise, was there not a reasonable chance that damage would be inflicted despite the presence of fighters ? It was decided to try. Wellingtons were deemed the most suitable aircraft for the purpose.

Owing, mainly, to poor visibility, it was not until 3rd December that twenty-four Wellingtons were at last able to discover a number of German warships off Heligoland. They attacked at heights varying between seven and ten thousand feet, using for the most part armour-piercing bombs. A stick of three scored hits on one of the larger ships, possibly the " Bremse " or the " Brummer," which was later seen down by the stern being towed to port. Photographs were taken, but cloud and the smoke from the explosions made accurate observation impossible. No damage was done by anti-aircraft fire from the ships, and of the

Crash-dive . . U-boat, caught on the surface by our bombers, attempts to crash-dive.

Not quick enough
A patch of oil and an eddy of foam remain

(Photographs taken by the aircraft which sank the submarine.

Seaplane base on Sylt. Hangars, Heinkel 59 seaplanes, and some He.115 seaplanes can be seen.

few enemy fighters which appeared, only one pressed home its attack and this was quickly shot down.

An unsuccessful attempt on the night of 27th/28th November was made by six "Whitleys," which flew through severe electrical storms, to reconnoitre Wilhelmshaven, Cuxhaven, Heligoland and Brunsbüttel. Twelve Wellingtons on the 14th December, however, found a German battleship, a cruiser and three destroyers some twelve miles south-west of Heligoland. To reach that point they had had to fly almost at sea level beneath low cloud, and when over the ships their height was not above 800 feet. They were immediately engaged by about twenty German fighters. The battle lasted forty minutes; and the Wellingtons, by maintaining formation, drove off the Messerschmitts, shot down five of them—of which three were 110's, met with for the first time in force—and damaged three more. Their own losses were five. Once again no definite conclusions could be drawn. True we had lost five aircraft, but it was almost certain that anti-aircraft fire from flak ships had accounted for three of these, while another had been the victim of a collision. The attack had not been carried out from high level as ordered, but from 800 feet because of the bad weather conditions. The encounter with the enemy fighters was on the whole distinctly encouraging. The crews of the Wellingtons were very well satisfied with the mutual fire power developed by the power-operated turrets. They had fought superior numbers with gallantry and resource. They had inflicted losses heavier than those which they had themselves sustained. It was decided to try the experiment once again.

The next opportunity came four days later, on 18th December, when a force of Wellingtons discovered a number of enemy naval units in Wilhelmshaven. Their adventures must be described in some detail, for several important lessons were learnt from this raid. The aircraft left in four formations with orders to bomb from a height not lower than 10,000 feet. The weather was bad to within fifty miles of the English coast, but the clouds gradually decreased until the sky was clear over the German coast. The first German fighters attacked a few miles south of Heligoland, but broke off as soon as the Wellingtons ran into heavy anti-aircraft fire in the neighbourhood of Bremerhaven. After that, very heavy fighter attacks were made upon them in the Wilhelmshaven area and continued until they were seventy to eighty miles out to sea on the way home. The visibility was so good that it was easy to see that there were no warships at Brunsbüttel, in the Schillig Roads or in the Jade Bay. The formation kept well to the east of Wilhelmshaven, but no target could be found. A sweep was therefore made over the Jade basin and course was then set directly for Wilhelmshaven, which was approached from the south-east. Enemy warships were, however, so close in to shore, some of them being at the quayside, that they could not be attacked without the risk of causing casualties among the civil population. Four large vessels, however, in the Roads, which opened heavy anti-aircraft fire, were attacked, without observed result.

Seeing no suitable targets, the leader of the formation turned north, past the Island of Wangerooge, at a height of 13,000 feet. No sooner had the heavy anti-aircraft fire died away than attacks by enemy fighters, which included Me.110's, ensued and were continued for about half an hour. The Wellingtons had, in fact, roused the hornets' nest and between forty and fifty attacks were delivered from astern and beam. The Me.110's opened fire with cannon at ranges of from 900 to 600 yards, and as a general rule pressed their attacks well home, coming on one occasion to within fifty yards. The action soon became general, the Wellingtons defending themselves with skill and vigour. Six Me.109's and six Me.110's were seen to fall in flames and six others probably suffered a similar fate. Four of the Wellingtons were reported to have been shot down, three made for Holland with petrol streaming from their tanks, and several others came down in the sea on the way home.

Certain incidents during the battle may be noted. There was the Wellington which was so heavily hit that all its gun turrets were put out of action. It escaped further damage and got safely home by taking up a position immediately below the remainder of the section which, flying in very close formation, successfully protected this defenceless aircraft from further enemy onslaught. Then there was the Wellington left behind in a turning movement. It was subjected to very heavy attack by enemy fighters. The centre turret and the wireless were put out of action and both the tail and front gunners were wounded. The second pilot, leaving his seat by the captain, took the place first of the wounded rear gunner, firing off all the ammunition, and then made his way along the lurching fuselage to the turret of the front gunner where he took like action. The pilot then dived to sea level and escaped.

Winter and Rough Weather

It had now become clear that we should have to accept heavy casualties if we attacked in daylight areas protected in strength by shore-based fighters.

These daylight attacks on ships in the German North Sea bases therefore gave way to sweeps over the North Sea by bombers on the look-out for enemy warships. They took place at frequent intervals whenever weather permitted and often when it did not. Thus, twenty-four Hampdens and eighteen Wellingtons sought vainly throughout the 21st December to find and bomb a large German warship, perhaps the "Deutschland," reported to be steaming north from the Great Belt. It was not found, but the operation showed that it was possible to maintain activity on a large scale even in extremely bad weather.

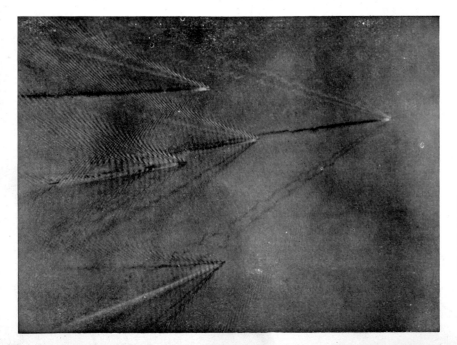

Enemy sortie. A bomber patrol sees German destroyers steaming off Heligoland, their bow and stern waves making herring-bone patterns.

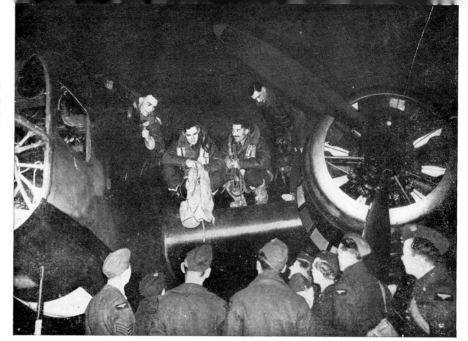

They accomplished much. They dared all. Bomber crew returned from a raid on a German North Sea base.

Further sweeps were carried out during the last days of that month and on a number of days in January and February, 1940. On 10th January a running fight between Blenheims and Me.110's took place a hundred miles off the German coast, with losses about equal on both sides. The weather grew more and more severe. On 11th February the Baltic was reported to be frozen from shore to shore. These conditions lasted more than a fortnight and reconnaissances were made at night to discover whether German warships were icebound in the neighbourhood of Heligoland. They were. On the night of 17th/18th a Whitley flying sometimes as low as 200 feet found four large warships two miles north-west of Heligoland and several cruisers and destroyers amounting to nine or ten ships four miles to the south-west. This was confirmed by further reconnaissances two nights later. Eighteen Wellingtons attacked at five-minute intervals, but once again, though bombs were dropped on the warships, the weather was too bad to make the operation successful. Nature, which had provided us with sitting targets, thought better of it and prevented us from attacking them.

Towards the end of October, 1939, the Germans began to use a new weapon with which to attack our shipping. This was the magnetic mine, and it was laid by aircraft as well as by other means. It was decided to make every effort to stop these mine-layers from taking off. They were at that time mostly seaplanes, He.115's, based on Borkum, Sylt and Norderney. Patrols were flown nightly in relays over these bases from 12th December. Their effect was to impose what amounted to a black-out. Any lights placed on the water to help seaplanes to take off in the dark were systematically bombed. The patrols were at once successful, for throughout the five nights from 12th to 16th December only one enemy aircraft was reported to be engaged in mine-laying. While this high rate of success was not always maintained, the patrols operated whenever they could. As an indication of their frequency it may be observed that forty-two sorties on Sylt and forty on Borkum were made between 12th December and the last night of the year.

These patrols went on until the attack on Sylt. This was carried out on the night of

19th/20th March, 1940. Thirty Whitleys and twenty Hampdens took part and the raid lasted about six hours. It was in the nature of a retort to the German raid on Scapa Flow three nights before. The weather was, as usual, poor with much fog, but there was moonlight over the target. Navigation was good, all but five aircraft arriving over the target in the order in which they left the ground. The bombs were dropped from heights varying from 10,000 to 1,000 feet. They consisted of 40 five-hundred pounders, 84 two-hundred-and-fifty pounders and about 1,200 incendiaries. The weight of bombs dropped would now seem very small. The Press, however, described it as a heavy raid and having regard to our operational strength in bombers at that time, this statement was true. The raid was in the nature of an experiment. The material damage caused was probably not as great as was originally estimated, but the lessons learned from this first attack at night on a land target by our bomber force were of more importance than the number of seaplanes, hangars and slip-ways damaged or destroyed.

IV—White Bombs :

THE LEAFLET RAIDS

September, 1939—still in progress

IN ADDITION to attacking the German Fleet when and where it could be found, our heavy bombers were given another task. It was to drop leaflets over Germany. Leaflets are part of the Government's propaganda campaign and have been used from the very outset of the war. The first leaflet raid was made on the night of 3rd/4th September when the conflict was not yet twelve hours old. Seven such raids took place on the first seven nights of the war. These preliminary operations were in the nature of an experiment, but by 16th September it was decided, in the light of experience gained, that they were a success and that the leaflet campaign should be carried on.

The justification for such a policy was twofold. Apart from the value in themselves of the pamphlets which were dropped—the first was a statement by the late Mr. Chamberlain, Prime Minister as he then was, setting forth the reasons why the British and French Empires were at war with Germany—the value to the Royal Air Force was very great. In the first place information about all kinds of objectives which might at any moment become the object of attack was obtained ; crews were able to become familiar with the whereabouts of aerodromes, factories, power stations, roads and railways in conditions very similar to those in which they were subsequently bombed. This information, combined with that obtained by the Advanced Air Striking Force in its reconnaissances over the western part of Germany, enabled a very complete picture to be built up for future use. Secondly, such raids proved of great importance in the training of air crews. They were carried out at night ; they were carried out in all weathers ; they lasted anything between six and twelve hours. As tests for navigation and endurance they had no equal.

Our bomber force was trained to operate both by day and by night. The duties of pamphlet dropping provided an excellent and unique method of continuing such training. Leaflet raids call for great endurance and sometimes an even higher degree of skill than bombing raids. A pilot taking a bomber to attack a target first flies to the area in which it is situated, and it is then pin-pointed for him by the navigator.

Leaflets are dropped through the flare-chute and scattered by the slip stream : in one type of bomber, now obsolescent, they were discharged from a gun-turret under the fuselage.

leaflets are packed in bundles secured by a piece of string which is cut before the bundle is pushed overboard. Once it enters the slip stream, the leaflets are scattered far and wide. On one occasion the dropper cut the string binding the bundles, not just before their discharge but just after they had been stowed in the aircraft. As it was taking off, a sudden draught papered its entire interior with leaflets which completely obscured the pilot's view. He had to make a blind take-off using only his instruments.

Bundles for Germany

The story of the early raids is soon told. The seven raids which took place in the first week of the war were followed by seven more during the month of September. The areas covered were the Ruhr and North-Western Germany. On the night of 1st/2nd October the first leaflet raid on Berlin took place. It was on that occasion that pamphlets were dropped giving the amount of the personal fortunes hidden away abroad by the Nazi leaders. Weather conditions that night were particularly severe. One aircraft arrived over the German capital at 22,500 feet. The oxygen supply momentarily failed ; two of the crew collapsed and part of the mechanism of the rear turret froze so that the air gunner could not open his door. The pilot carried on and the navigator went back to assist the two unconscious members of the crew. He dragged one twelve feet along the fuselage into the cabin and connected him with the oxygen supply. He then threw overboard two-thirds of the leaflets before collapsing in his turn. The pilot brought the aircraft down to 9,000 feet, and at this height it became possible to open the door of the rear turret. The air gunner climbed through to the assistance of the navigator, who,

The target itself is of limited proportions. In the case of leaflets, however, what is aimed at is the wide area occupied by a whole town or district. The direction and strength of the wind and the height at which the aircraft is flying assume much greater importance when leaflets instead of bombs are to be dropped. The leaflet, lighter than the bomb, is carried by the wind. Experiments were made to find out what was the most suitable wind strength so that an ideal wind could be discovered. The leaflets were released at various distances and heights. This technique had to be learnt and it was not learnt in a night. On several occasions in the early days leaflets fell on countries then neutral, such as Holland, Belgium and Denmark. On the whole, however, comparatively few mistakes were made.

Our bombers were not equipped for their discharge and they had to be dropped by hand through the flare-chute which was specially adapted for the purpose. The

however, had already recovered and returned to duty. It may be noted that all the aircraft engaged in this operation left at three-minute intervals and returned at the same intervals, a remarkable feat of navigation and timing.

Besides this raid on Berlin leaflets were dropped on eight more occasions in the month of October by aircraft operating mostly from the French aerodrome of Villeneuve. The night of 27th/28th October, 1939, is noteworthy because of the appalling weather conditions encountered. These were such that " it caused much amazement "—so the official report runs—" when it was realised that aircraft in such a condition of ' icing-up ' could still be controlled."

The adventures of the Whitley crews, all of whom succeeded in dropping their load of pamphlets in the Dusseldorf-Frankfurt area, were numerous. One difficulty was common to them all. It was almost impossible to lower the turret from which the pamphlets were discharged owing to the intense cold. The temperature varied between minus 22 and minus 32° centigrade. In one aircraft the starboard engine had to be switched off because it had caught fire. At that time the aircraft was in thick cloud, and ice about 6 inches thick formed on its wings. It went into a dive and " *recovery was made at 7,000 feet, the full strength of both pilots being required to pull the aircraft out of the dive. It was then found that the rudder and elevators were immovable. The wireless operator sent a signal to say one engine was on fire and tried to get an immediate ' fix ' but had no means of knowing if he was transmitting as the instrument glasses were thick with ice.*

" *The aircraft at this stage was on an even keel but losing height at 2,000 feet per minute. The port engine had stopped, and we observed some 4 inches of ice protruding from the inside of the engine cowling. The airscrew,*

Operation successful. The crew clamber out of their aircraft. Leaflet raids were severe tests of navigational skill and endurance.

leading edges and windscreens were covered thickly with ice. The order was given to abandon aircraft by parachute ; but as no reply was forthcoming from the front and rear gunners, the order was immediately cancelled. It was afterwards ascertained that the front gunner was unconscious due to a blow on the head from an ammunition magazine, and the rear gunner was unconscious from a blow on the head from the turret due to the dive and subsequent recovery. The aircraft then assumed a shallow high-speed dive. We opened the top hatch to see where we were going, and the second pilot, who was at the controls, opened the side window. The aircraft emerged from the clouds in heavy rain at about 200 feet above the ground. All we could see was a black forest with a grey patch in the middle, for which we were heading ; the second pilot pulled the aircraft over the trees brushing through their tops, and the aircraft dropped flat into a field, travelled through a wire fence, skidded broadside on and came to rest with the port wing against the trees on the further side of the clearing.

" It was then found that the starboard engine was on fire which was increasing in severity. We climbed out and attempted to put out the flames, but were unsuccessful. The captain returned to the fuselage to get the extinguisher but found it had already discharged in the crash. On seeing the fire the wireless operator obtained the extinguisher from his cabin, climbed on to the engine cowling and extinguished the flames. We then ascertained that all members of the crew were safe and unhurt." They were subsequently succoured by the local inhabitants, who were fortunately French, though not until they had spent the night in the crashed Whitley.

In another Whitley a defect in the oxygen apparatus caused a shortage of supply. The crew, however, succeeded in dropping their pamphlets, but " such was the condition of the navigator and wireless operator at this stage, that every few minutes they were compelled to lie down and rest on the floor of the fuselage. The cockpit heating system was useless. Everyone was frozen, and had no means of alleviating their distress. The navigator and Commanding Officer were butting their heads on the floor and navigation table in an endeavour to experience some other form of pain as a relief from the awful feeling of frost-bite and lack of oxygen." On the way home they descended to 8,000 feet, but icing conditions grew worse. The windows became completely covered, " and ice could be heard coming off the blades of the airscrews and striking the sides of the nose. Continuous movement of the controls was necessary to prevent them from freezing up." Nevertheless the aircraft landed safely.

" Successful Avoiding Action "

The remaining Whitley engaged in this operation also made a forced landing in France. The landing was particularly heavy and the tail gunner was much shaken. When after climbing out he went to the nose of the aircraft to have a word with the pilot, he discovered that he was alone, the others having on the orders of the captain baled out. Owing to a breakdown in the intercommunication system the tail gunner had not received this order. The aircraft had made a landing by itself with no one at the controls. The tail gunner went off to a near-by village : here he found the rest of the crew safe in a café, where they exchanged experiences. The front gunner had been knocked unconscious by his parachute which, when opening, hit him on the head. He regained consciousness lying on his back in a field among a herd of curious but friendly cows. The wireless operator was not so lucky. Landing in a field full of curious but hostile bulls, he took successful avoiding action by sprinting for the hedge in full flying kit and cleared a four-foot hurdle. The captain landed softly and was unhurt, and the navigator sprained an ankle. It is pleasant to record that the whole crew after their re-union in the café were taken, " complete with bouquets," to a French hospital, whence, after treatment, they returned the same day to their Unit.

In January, 1940, the raids which took place between 7th and 14th were of importance, for they afforded an opportunity of recon-noitring the area along the Dutch and Belgian frontiers. On the night of 12th/13th the first leaflet raid on Prague and Vienna was made. This was a long flight which took units of the Royal Air Force into the heart of the enemy's territory. The air-craft, three of them, took off shortly before five in the afternoon. They crossed the German frontier near Karlsruhe at 14,000 feet, and their next main landmark was Munich, which was clearly visible. The Bavarian Alps were then crossed, " their snow-clad peaks showing up magnificently in the starry night." On reaching Vienna pam-phlets were dropped and " after circling the city, which was a mass of twinkling lights reflected from the black waters of the Danube," the aircraft set a course for their base, which was reached safely in the early hours of the morning of the 13th. The average temperature throughout the flight was minus 20° centigrade.

Owing to very bad weather the raids were only on a small scale in January and up to 25th February. On that date and for five successive nights leaflets were dropped in the Berlin area and in the Hamburg, Bremen, Kiel, Lübeck, Cologne and Rhineland areas. On 5th, 6th and 7th March leaflet raids were pushed as far as the Posen area, and on 9th to Czechoslovakia. A leaflet raid on 7th March over the Rhine and the Ruhr was of particular value. The glow of the blast-furnaces was easily seen and their whereabouts were noted.

On the night of 15th/16th March came the longest raid of all. Two Whitleys went to Warsaw and dropped between 6,000,000 and 7,000,000 leaflets. On the return journey one aircraft landed in France, the other behind the lines in Germany. The crew, thinking that they were safely over the border in friendly territory, left the Whitley, the pilot having locked the controls. It was then near dawn. Peasants, when asked at what place the aircraft had landed, greeted the crew with laughter when they discovered that the British airmen imagined that they were in France. By gestures the peasants explained that France was a short distance away across the wooded hills. The atmos-phere continued to be cordial, but a number of soldiers presently appeared on bicycles. Maintaining their friendly attitude towards the peasants the crew of the Whitley gradually edged away and then made a bolt for it. The soldiers opened rifle fire upon them, but they reached their aircraft in safety, took off, and on the few gallons of petrol remaining succeeded in reaching France.

In these early raids opposition was on the whole slight. Anti-aircraft fire was seldom encountered, but a certain number of German night fighters sought to intercept our bombers. They were sometimes successful, but such casualties as were suffered were due mostly to the very bad weather conditions in which many of the flights were made. On one occasion an Me.109 attacked a Whitley and closed to within 500 yards. The rear gunner duly reported the presence of the enemy aircraft just as the captain had given orders for the leaflets to be dropped. He told the rear gunner to hold his fire while the navigator and wireless operator continued to throw them out. The rear gunner presently reported that it would not be necessary for him to take any action since the Me.109 had flown into the cloud of released leaflets and dived away discomfited.

Leaflet raids continued on a fairly wide scale up to the beginning of the attack on Norway. They are still carried out, but now the load of the aircraft also includes bombs.

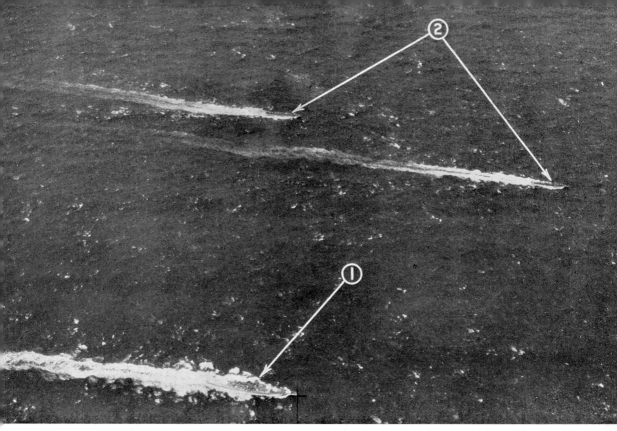

"The German Fleet was a grand sight." 1, The "Gneisenau" heading towards Norway. 2, Part of her destroyer screen.

V—Campaign Against Odds:

NORWAY

9th April—10th May, 1940

ALTHOUGH it was not until 9th April, 1940, that German ships of war were seen in Norwegian harbours, they had sailed two days earlier on the 7th. On the 8th Denmark was invaded and overrun. Four days previously, on 4th April, a reconnaissance flight over the Elbe estuary discovered German naval vessels and some sixty merchant ships in the Schillig Roads moving northward in formations of five ships. The naval vessels were attacked by six Blenheims without visible result. A patrol sent to the same place on the next day had to be recalled on account of weather ; but its leader got through and flying just below clouds, which were down to 200 feet, found the Roads almost empty. On Saturday, 6th April, a photographic reconnaissance showed that several units of the German Fleet, including the "Scharnhorst" and the "Gneisenau", were in the harbours of North-Western Germany. It was, however, on the night of 6th/7th April that the signs of an impending great event became unmistakable. British bombers engaged in the dropping of leaflets reported that a wide stream of motor transport, headlights blazing, was flowing along the *Autobahn* from Hamburg to Lübeck, while at Eckernforde, near Kiel, there was great activity among shipping under the glare of brilliant arc lamps. The Germans made no pretence of concealment. When all is on the hazard they rarely do, believing that speed is more important than secrecy.

On 7th April, the importance of speed in the transmission of messages was well illustrated. Twelve Blenheims in two formations of six saw an enemy cruiser and four destroyers at sea. They followed them and four minutes later caught sight of most of the German Fleet, which was then some seventy-six miles N.N.W. of the Horn's Reef. The Blenheims wheeled into the sun and attacked either the " Scharnhorst " or the " Gneisenau." The leader sent out a message giving the position and course of the German Fleet. This information never got through and only became known some hours later when the aircraft returned. " *The German Fleet was a very grand sight,*" said the leader of the Blenheims. " *When they shot at me it was like lightning flashing in daylight all about me.*"

Wellingtons sought in vain to find the German ships that same afternoon, and another force detailed for the same task the next day were weather-bound ; but on 9th April twelve Wellingtons and twelve Hampdens went out to attack the enemy naval forces now in Bergen. They arrived at dusk and dropped their bombs with some effect, for they obtained two direct hits on a cruiser. This was subsequently sunk in a very gallant attack made the next day by sixteen Skuas of the Fleet Air Arm.

Not a Base, Not a Chance

By now the Luftwaffe had arrived in force in Norway. They concentrated on the aerodrome and seaplane anchorage at Stavanger, the aerodrome at Vaernes, near Trondheim and also on Fornebu, the airport of Oslo. The first landings of air-borne troops on that aerodrome were made regardless of cost in lives and aircraft ; and the manœuvre succeeded. In order to maintain the rate of landings, the Germans by 15th April were using passenger aircraft taken from their Continental passenger services. Together with the German ships at Bergen, Kristiansand, Trondheim and elsewhere the newly-occupied aerodromes formed the most obvious targets for Bomber Command.

Lack of cloud cover on 11th April prevented a force of Hampdens from attacking warships in Kristiansand South ; but that night more than forty of our heavy bombers attacked German shipping *en route* from Kiel to Oslo. Heavy darkness hampered the operation. One ship, however, was seen to explode with great violence. On 12th April a great effort was made to bomb some of the main units of the German Fleet. These included the " Scharnhorst," the " Gneisenau " and a cruiser of the " Nürnberg " class which had been discovered heading south across the entrance to the Skagerrak. Ninety-two heavy bombers swept a wide area in search of these vessels. There was fog about and they were not seen, but two warships in Kristiansand South were bombed. The Wellingtons and Hampdens detailed for the operation presently found themselves heavily engaged by a swarm of Me.109's and 110's, which pursued them 200 miles out to sea. In this running fight ten of our aircraft were lost. Two Me.110's were seen to be shot down ; but the Germans admitted the destruction of five Me.109's. Our losses were probably greater in numbers and certainly in trained airmen than were theirs.

The concentration of our attacks soon came to be upon Stavanger. It was, from the start, the main German air base in Norway from which their attacks on our shipping soon developed. We attacked it first towards dusk on 11th April. Two Blenheim fighters sprayed the aerodrome with machine-gun fire. They were followed by six Wellingtons which delivered a low-level attack, starting a large fire. As the campaign went on it became increasingly clear that the only really effective action which the Royal Air Force could take against the enemy was to attack Stavanger repeatedly in the hope that its continued use might be curtailed. A glance at the map will show how difficult it was to do more.

The shortest distance between the coasts of Norway and the British Isles varies between three and four hundred miles. Every yard is open sea. Since we had no bases in Norway itself, our bombers had to fly all that way and back in each operation they undertook. This meant heavy loads of petrol and consequently smaller loads of bombs. Moreover the time they could afford to spend over the target, if they were to make sure of getting back to base, was very short.

The support which they could give to our army when it had landed was therefore strictly limited. Had Trondheim with its aerodrome at Vaernes been captured, the course of the campaign might well have been different; but it remained in enemy hands and no other air bases were available for bombers. It was, therefore, impossible to provide that continuous and prolonged air support which the Army so urgently needed. To have done so from bases in England and Scotland a force at least as large as the whole German Luftwaffe would not have been too much. Such a force did not exist.

In Norway, as in Greece and later on in Crete, the advantage lay all with the enemy. He had obtained the aerodromes of Denmark without resistance. He had secured those of Norway with scarcely greater difficulty, for his attack had been as swift as it had been treacherous and the Norwegian resistance was paralysed from the outset. Once established, it was impossible to dislodge

" Back from Bergen." The crews of two of the Hampden bombers which attacked German fleet concentrations in Bergen Fjord. Two direct hits were registered on a German cruiser.

him.   Aerodromes such as Fornebu, near
Oslo, were outside the range of all but our
long-distance bombers, the Whitleys, which
could not operate in daylight without running
the almost certain risk of being shot down.

"Where is the —— place ? "

There have been many references to the
weather in this account.   Through all the
early months of the war and especially during
the Norwegian campaign it remained a
factor of cardinal importance, and it must not
be forgotten that in April it is still winter in
Norway.   To illustrate the appalling weather
met with, here is an account by the pilot of
a Blenheim, one of those which attacked
Stavanger on 16th April.

" *Soon after leaving the English coast,*" he
said, " *we ran into rain which was literally
tropical in its fury.   After some time we climbed
and then the rain turned to snow.   At* 13,000
*feet the engines of two of the Blenheims became
iced up and stopped.   One of the aircraft
dropped more or less out of control until only
600 feet above the sea, when they started
again.   The other Blenheim was even luckier.
It actually struck the waves at the very
moment its engines came to life.   It lost its
rear wheel, but both aircraft got safely back
to base.*"   In such conditions it is not surprising that only one of that formation of
Blenheims reached Stavanger.   It was flying
very low and a brisk argument was in progress
between the pilot and the observer as to
their whereabouts.   " *Call yourself an observer,*" said the pilot.   " *Where is the ——
place ?* "   At that moment a piece of anti-
aircraft shell removed half the cowling of his
cockpit.   They knew they had arrived.

Stavanger was bombed sixteen times by
aircraft of Bomber Command between 11th
and 24th April.   It was also heavily shelled
by H.M.S. " Suffolk " at dawn on the 17th
besides being repeatedly attacked by aircraft
of Coastal Command and by the Fleet Air

Arm.   The damage done was considerable,
especially on the 15th.   The best attack from
a tactical point of view was probably that
carried out by twelve Blenheims on the 17th.
They flew in two formations at different
heights.   The high-flying formation dropped
their bombs ten seconds before those flying
at a lower level went in to the attack.   By
keeping formation they drove off repeated
attacks by enemy fighters, though two,
which became stragglers, were cut off and
shot down.   Many other attacks on Stavanger
were made during the rest of April and
the first week of May.   That on the night of
2nd/3rd May was probably the most successful.

Since the German occupation of Norway,
aerodromes at Kristiansand, Oslo, Stavanger
and Trondheim have been attacked twice,
nine, seventeen and five times respectively
up to the middle of June, 1941.   In the
opening month of the campaign Fornebu
was attacked whenever possible.   At the
end of April it was bombed four times
in four days.   It was always, however, a
target very hard to find.   Why this was so
can be realised from what happened to a
Whitley which set out to attack it and
neighbouring occupied aerodromes on the
night of 16th/17th April, 1940.

At dusk on 16th April, the Commanding
Officer of one of our bomber squadrons took
off from his base in Yorkshire as captain
of a Whitley.   Amongst the members of his
crew, his navigator and second pilot were
new to the work—the former making his
first war flight.   Clouds were low at the
start, but the pilot climbed to 11,000 feet
into a moderately clear layer between upper
and lower cloud masses.   Setting a course
for the southern promontory of Norway to
establish a landfall, and flying by dead
reckoning, they made the sea crossing at
10,000 feet.   Owing to cloud the coast-line
was missed and the first sight the pilot had
of land was when, shortly after 11 p.m., a
snow-covered hill appeared in the bright

Stavanger Aerodrome, a key point in the German occupation of Norway. 1, Runways. 2, Two aircraft in head-on collision. 3, Aircraft with port wing broken. 4, Stacks of stores.

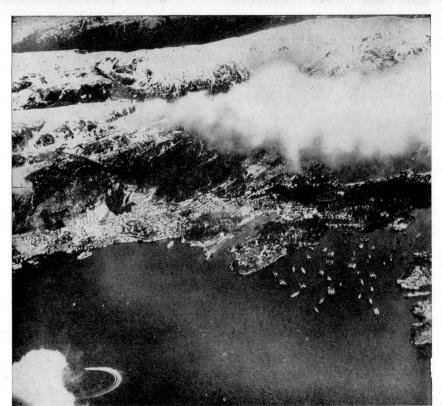

Bergen. In the left-hand bottom corner an E-boat takes avoiding action as our aircraft sweep over. A warehouse and supply ship, hit during a previous raid, can be seen still burning in the centre bay.

End of a Dornier. A Dornier 18 flying boat, shot down by aircraft of Bomber Command, lying crippled in the sea off Norway.

moonlight through a gap in the clouds. Recognising the rolling nature of the country, the pilot fixed his position and set a course to cut the south-east coast of Norway in order to make a landfall. Once again the coast was missed. Half an hour later, driving through a gap at 3,000 feet, a flat black surface was seen. The pilot could not determine whether it was land or water. He therefore switched on his landing light and flew down its beam until the reflection revealed the sea. Course was altered to port until the coast-line was picked up at 2,000 feet and identified by the foam of breakers.

For the next half-hour the pilot, with his face pressed into the open aperture of his cockpit window, picked his way in and out of cloud, along the intricate coast to the entrance of Oslo Fjord. Continuing in this manner he reached Drammen at 1,500 feet. Great activity was observed alongside the docks on the southern banks of Drammen Fjord. At least ten cargo vessels of all sizes were seen alongside, and numerous other ships were moored in the entrance to the fjord. The docks were floodlit and riding lights were displayed. Tempting though this target was, the pilot's task was to find and attack Oslo aerodrome. So, retracing his path, he set a course for the Norwegian capital at 3,000 feet.

At the head of the Oslo Fjord a severe snowstorm was encountered. The aerodrome at Fornebu and the surrounding country were completely obscured. Several attempts were made to penetrate the gloom, the aircraft coming down to a height of 500 feet where it at once met with severe icing conditions. The pilot therefore flew back over enemy shipping in Drammen in the hope that the snowstorm would abate. In this he was disappointed and, although Oslo was bathed in bright moonlight, the area of the landing grounds was still invisible. It might have been possible to judge the position of the target in relation to the town ; but rather than risk the destruction of non-military objectives the pilot set a course for England, his bombs still on board. He landed safely at his base shortly after 4.30 in the morning, after being in the air for nine and a half hours. No wireless " fixes " were asked for or received throughout the flight.

Dress Rehearsal

In addition to bombing attacks, reconnaissance flights by all classes of bomber aircraft were made throughout the active period of the Norwegian campaign. The whereabouts of German shipping off the coasts of Germany, in the Belt, in Oslo Fjord and in the numerous fjords on the west coast of Norway were plotted, and much valuable information made available for the Royal Navy.

Through this period of just one month, Bomber Command was hard-worked, four squadron sorties in six days being nothing unusual. The losses were some thirty bombers.

More might, perhaps, have been accomplished, but the task was from the outset of the most formidable kind. There was no more than a small force of bombers available, and it had to operate at extreme range in thick weather, without fighter support and with information always inadequate and sometimes altogether lacking. Bomber Command did its utmost. All flights were carried out in the spirit of the crew of the Wellington who flew, at 300 feet through fierce snowstorms, from the north to the south of Norway and back to Scotland in fourteen and a half hours. The spirit of our pilots and crews was, indeed, as high at the end of those thirty days as it had been at the beginning.

Though they did not know it at the time, for most of them the campaign was a dress rehearsal for what they were about to be called upon to do over Holland, Belgium and France.

VI—Western Front:

THE BATTLE OF FLANDERS

10th May—15th June, 1940

ON 10TH MAY, 1940, the Germans attacked Holland, Belgium and France simultaneously. For the sake of clarity their operations against the Dutch must first be briefly outlined.

They opened by a bombing attack on the Schipol aerodrome, the barracks at Amsterdam and the anti-aircraft defences nearby. This was soon followed by the descent of parachute troops on key points in and near The Hague, at Delft, Zandvoord, the Hook, Ymuiden, Eindhoven, Dordrecht and on the Waalhaven aerodrome near Rotterdam. They succeeded in capturing the aerodrome. By the afternoon of 10th May four major aerodromes in Fortress Holland, those at Waalhaven, Ypenburg, Ockenburg and Walkenburg were in German hands, despite the measures taken to deny their use to the invader. The Germans at once began to land troops in large numbers from troop-carrying aircraft. Two or three aerodromes were subsequently recaptured by the Dutch and held for a short period. German aircraft also landed in considerable numbers on the foreshore at Katwijk, Scheveningen and Wassenaar. The result of these air operations was to immobilise one Dutch army corps in Fortress Holland and to secure for the Germans control of the district of Dordrecht and the southern part of Rotterdam. The effect on the general campaign in Holland was decisive.

The Royal Air Force immediately gave all the aid it could to the hard-pressed Dutch. This record deals only with the part played in it by Bomber Command. Its aircraft were in action within a few hours, but their task was very heavy. The main armies of Belgium, Great Britain and France were hotly engaged with the German invading forces and needed all the help—and more —that it was possible to give. Nevertheless the Dutch were not left to fight in the air unaided. On 10th May many bombing attacks were carried out on Dutch aerodromes in German hands and on the Dutch beaches, the most considerable being those on the Waalhaven and Ypenburg aerodromes, on a landing ground near Leyden and on the foreshore near The Hague. Considerable damage was done for the loss of four Blenheims. That night thirty-six Wellingtons burnt the hangars at Waalhaven and destroyed a large number of enemy aircraft on the ground, while a squadron of Whitleys bombed the approaches to Maastricht. A further attack was made on the same area on 11th May, and on 13th and 14th May the area round Breda was bombed by Battles from the Advanced Air Striking Force in France and by Blenheims from England. Great stocks of oil were set on fire.

Throughout the few days of the campaign, Bomber Command were constantly hampered as in Norway by lack of information on the situation. This made the allotment of targets a matter of extreme difficulty. So great was the confusion prevailing that on one occasion at least we bombed Ypenburg aerodrome at the request of the Dutch Government, although at that moment, unknown to them and to ourselves, it had been regained temporarily by Dutch troops. Our bombing attacks, determined though they were, could not greatly influence the fate of Holland. The number of German aircraft was overwhelming. There were so many that Göring could afford to disregard losses. Sheer weight of numbers achieved

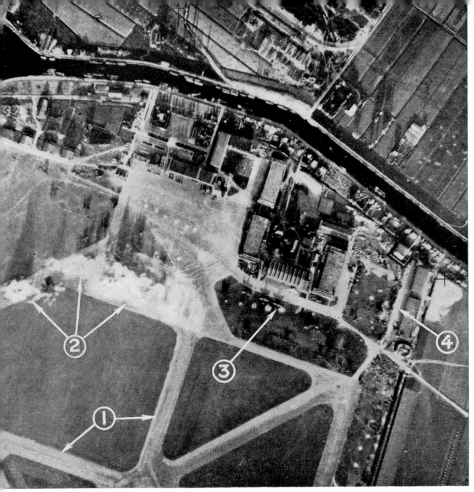

once more what it had already accomplished in Poland and Norway. The Dutch Air Force fought with all the stubborn fury for which the men of the Low Countries are justly renowned. It was wiped out in three days. By 13th May, only 10 of the 248 aircraft which went into action on 10th survived and by the evening of that day those 10 had been destroyed in an attack on German formations behind the Grebbe line.

Meanwhile the battle was joined in Belgium and France. Before tracing the fortunes of our bomber forces during its progress, the use to which they were to be put must be considered. There are two direct ways in which a bombing force can aid an army on the defensive. It can interfere with the enemy's lines of communications by bombing railways, roads, points of assembly, "bottle-necks," dumps, etc., and it can also in certain circumstances give close support by bombing enemy troops engaged in close action. These possible uses for the British bombing force had been carefully considered and discussed with the French as far back as the spring of 1939, when the seizure by Hitler of Czechoslovakia had made the prospect of a German attack in the West almost inevitable.

At that time the French General Staff were informed without reserve what our strength in bombers was. Plans, based on that strength, were drawn up and accepted by both allies without reserve. The French General Staff made it clear at the outset that their main preoccupation was the invasion of their country. They viewed with the greatest misgiving any plan by which bombers were to be used for attacks on German industry and they did not hesitate to say so. In their considered opinion the main, indeed the only, use to which a bombing force should be put was to extend the range of artillery supporting armies in the field. They therefore pressed from the start for the full co-operation of the whole British bomber force in resisting any German invasion of France. This was immediately promised. It was made clear that Great Britain would regard the defeat of the invasion of France as her primary task and that her bomber force would be used to the utmost to help in fulfilling it. At the same time the French General Staff were warned not to expect any very spectacular result from bomber support, since the enemy was superior in numbers and most of our bomber bases were separated by great distances from the area of the battlefield.

The French were deeply impressed with the importance of bombing railways. The disruption of enemy communications appeared to them to be the best way in which the bombing force could be of real help. It was pointed out to them that only a strictly limited result could be expected from such a bombardment. It was, for example, useless to bomb anything but junctions and other points vital to the railway transport system of Germany. Moreover, such points would have to be kept under more or less constant attack. This would have required a bomber force vastly larger than that at the disposal of the Allies. The French General Staff also wished aerodromes to be bombed with the object of making so many holes in them that they would become unusable. They were not impressed by our contention that this was not an effective or an economical method of " grounding " the German Air Force, all the more so when the large number of aerodromes available to the enemy was taken into consideration.

Matters stood thus when war broke out. We immediately fulfilled our promises and despatched the Advanced Air Striking Force, consisting of most of our medium bomber squadrons then armed mainly with Battles, to the Rheims area. This force must not be confused with the Air Component, which consisted of a number of fighter, army co-operation and reconnaissance squadrons operating directly under the orders of the Commander-in-Chief of the British Expeditionary Force. The area of Rheims was chosen for the Striking Force because the Battle possessed a comparatively short range and had, therefore, to be placed as close as possible to objectives in Germany. The Battles were also regarded as being the most suitable aircraft available for the direct support of the French army in the event of an invasion. They were put into use for reconnaissance purposes almost immediately. Very early in the war General Gamelin mounted a strictly limited offensive on the Saar front. He asked for the support of the Advanced Air Striking Force and this was at once given.

Here an immediate difficulty arose. For a bomber force to carry out its duties with the

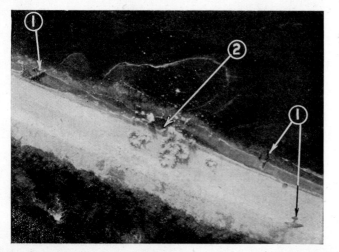

German aircraft landed on the foreshore at Katwijk at the beginning of the invasion of Holland (10th May, 1940). 1, Ju.52 troop-carrying aircraft on the sandy beach. 2, Bombs bursting.

maximum of efficiency, an elaborate and detailed ground organisation for its direction and control is necessary. Such organisation did not exist in France and was only established by the British Air Staff after many technical difficulties had been overcome. One other point is of importance. The French said definitely that they could not undertake any day bombing by their own air force. Since they did not possess more than forty day bombers this attitude was not surprising. Their aircraft industry, which went into full production much later than our own, concentrated, naturally enough, on the building of fighter aircraft. Great Britain, faced with this deficiency in the French bombing forces, agreed at once and without hesitation to use the Advanced Air Striking Force to bomb the German armies if it became necessary to do so.

The operations of that force prior to 10th May, 1940, consisted entirely of reconnaissance duties. Flights were made by night and day over Germany, but the Battles did not penetrate more than twenty miles into enemy territory. The photographs they took enabled an accurate picture of the Siegfried Line to be built up. They bore their full share with the French Air Force in the limited offensive operations, already mentioned, undertaken against the Saar. It was during the course of these that on 30th September, 1939, four out of five Battles were shot down in a fight with fifteen Messerschmitts over Saarbrücken. Most of their crews escaped by parachute after having accounted for two of the enemy.

Matters continued thus until the German offensive against France began. In the meantime, however, the attack on Norway had ꜱed the French High Command to raise ꞓ again the question of the use to be made ur bombing force. On 14th April that mand was informed that, subject to a mini-diversion to Norway, Denmark and ern Germany, it was intended, should

the Germans attack, to use our full offensive strength in the area of the enemy's advance and in the districts east of the Rhine through which his lines of communication and supply would have to run. On the next day the *Comité de Guerre* ruled that, because casualties might be caused to the civilian population, bombing attacks on enemy concentrations in Germany were not to be made unless the Germans launched them upon the Allies. This decision at once limited the possible objectives to enemy columns on the march. It was pointed out to General Gamelin that such targets were quite unsuitable for our heavy bombers, since they had been designed for an entirely different purpose. General Gamelin remained unconvinced. The German attack opened in force on 10th May, 1940. The Allied Commander-in-Chief still refused to allow objectives in Germany or German troops on the move in their own country to be bombed. It was not until the afternoon of the 10th that the Advanced Air Striking Force bombed German columns advancing through Luxembourg and not until the next day that attacks were made on enemy troops and lines of communication by our medium and heavy bombing forces.

Delaying Action

The task of the British bombers now that the battle was joined can be summed up in a sentence. It was to delay and weaken in every way possible the advance of the German mechanised forces and, after these had scored their initial successes, to try to relieve the pressure on the Allied armies sufficiently to enable them first to hold the enemy and then to mount an effective counter-attack. This delaying action by our bombers had been carefully planned. An analysis of German communications and possible lines of advance into Holland and Belgium had been made and the places where these would cross water or some other obstacle had been tabulated. Special maps had been prepared and issued to the British and French Air Forces. By a system of secret reference points they enabled the bombers of either force to be easily and rapidly directed by means of a signal to any area or objective at will.

The centre of gravity, the direction and the extent of the enemy's advance were discovered by reconnaissance; and the information thus obtained, combined with the delay imposed on the enemy by all arms, of which the bombers may have been the most important, enabled the French armies to reach and establish themselves in their previously selected positions north of the River Meuse.

In fulfilment of the general plan, the heavy bombers were used at night on the enemy's communications and supply centres, while the Advanced Air Striking Force operated in daylight until its casualties became too severe. Its task was to carry out low-flying attacks against enemy columns, road junctions and railways. It went into action immediately. While in the Maastricht area the Blenheims made numerous attacks on the crossing over the Meuse and on troops advancing along the road to Tongres, the Battles bombed enemy columns, which were discovered on the move through Luxembourg. The casualties they inflicted were heavy, but they lost nearly half their number, mostly to anti-aircraft fire. They were to lose many more by the action of enemy fighters. The heaviest casualties were suffered on the 12th, 14th and 17th May.

Breaking the Bridges

To understand the operations of our bombing forces, it is necessary to refer from time to time to the progress and direction of the German thrusts on land. These were powerful and continuous. By mid-day on 10th May the Germans had held up the French attempt to advance in Southern Luxembourg and were pressing on into Belgium over undestroyed bridges near Maastricht. They had captured Fort Eben Emael by parachute troops and were thus threatening Liége. On the 11th they attacked the Albert Canal position in flank with mechanised divisions coming from Aix-la-Chapelle and in front with troops which crossed the northern part of Dutch Limburg and moved on Hasselt. Matters stood thus when on 12th May it was learned that two bridges across the Albert Canal to the west of Maastricht had not been destroyed and that the enemy was pouring across them. A squadron of Blenheims was detailed to bomb the crossings. They delivered their attack from 3,000 feet in the face of very heavy anti-aircraft fire. Their experienced leader afterwards described it as the heaviest he had not only encountered but imagined. On approaching the target the squadron broke formation in order to run in upon it from several directions. The bombs were falling when the leader spotted enemy fighters about to attack out of the sun. He immediately called on his squadron to regain formation, a manœuvre of great difficulty and danger because of the heavy anti-aircraft fire. They did so at once and faced the fighters, which were driven off by their concentrated fire. Eight out of the twelve Blenheims, every one of them hit, returned, their task accomplished. The same objectives were also attacked on that day by six Battles. The crews which manned them were chosen by lot, since everyone had volunteered. They went in low, disregarding the enemy fighters above and the A.A. fire below. Five of the six were shot down. The sixth crashed on fire inside our lines the pilot having instructed his crew to ju One end of the bridge was demolished. Victoria Crosses were awarded to the of the leading Battle.

The bridges were temporarily ou

Broken Bridges. A photograph illustrating the great importance of bridge demolition; enemy traffic is delayed and restricted by the work of the Allied sappers at Maastricht. 1, Road bridges under repair. 2, Bombs bursting along the bank of the Meuse. 3, Wrecked span of railway bridge. 4, Póntoon bridge built by the Germans. 5, German transport parked in, and 6, making a detour through, the town. The bridges bombed by the R.A.F. were over the Albert Canal, to the west of the Meuse.

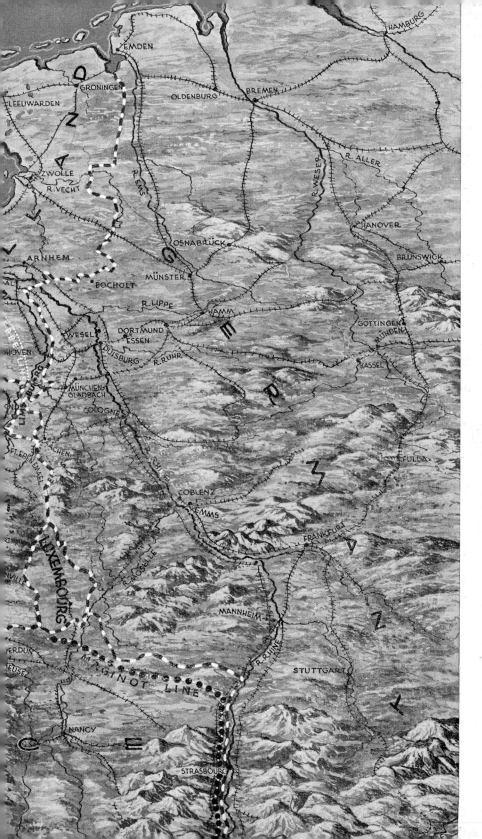

**THE CAMPAIGN
IN FLANDERS**

The area over which
Bomber Command
operated in resisting
the German attack
on Holland, Belgium
and Northern France

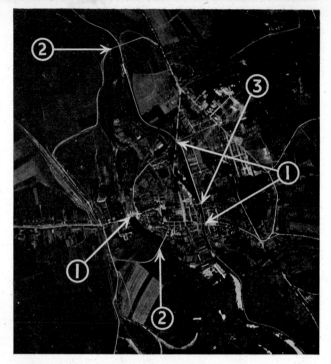

Bridges over the Meuse at Mouzon (above) and Sedan (below) were the target of heroic attacks by our Battles on 14th May, 1940. Most of the bridges had already been destroyed by Allied sappers: but our aircraft hit two permanent and several pontoon bridges. 1, Broken bridges. 1a, Bridge damaged by bombing. 2. New bridges. 3, Pontoon bridge.

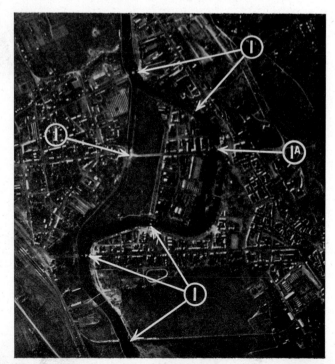

action, but this did not suffice to stop the German advance. By the close of that day, heavy fighting was going on in the Ardennes and the Belgian Army had been forced to retire from Tongres. On the 13th they had retreated some twenty miles in the direction of Tirlemont. Attacks on Longwy at the northern end of the Maginot Line had, however, been repulsed by the French. The British Army, together with much of the French group of Northern armies, had made contact with the right of the Belgian line. Next day, the 14th, was disastrous to the Allies. The Germans broke the French Ninth Army defending the Meuse and crossed the river, thus making a breach in the line between Sedan and Dinant. This meant that the Allied armies in Eastern Belgium were in imminent peril of being outflanked.

The Germans crossed the Meuse at two places, one of them near Sedan. At first it seemed possible to destroy the bridges they were using with a comparatively small force of aircraft. Six Battles made the first attack about 5 a.m. All returned, the pilot of one being wounded. Shortly after about 7.30 a.m., the attacks were renewed by four more Battles, and hits were claimed on a pontoon bridge near Sedan. All four got back safely. The situation, however, continued to deteriorate, and by 2 p.m. a much larger force was standing by to attack this and four other bridges between Mouzon and Sedan. Sixty-seven Battles started off soon after 3 p.m. Thirty-two returned. The rest had fallen victims to intense A.A. fire and to the German fighters, which were so numerous that they could not all be driven away. Two pontoon bridges were destroyed, another damaged, and two permanent bridges —one at Mouzon, the other at Sedan itself— received direct hits. During the days following, six crews of the Battles filtered back to their base. These included a pilot, wounded in two places, who yet succeeded in swimming the Meuse, and an observer and an air gunner who had tended their wounded pilot for more than twenty-four hours, only leaving him when he died. They also got across the Meuse to safety.

These and other attacks of a similar kind showed that, when a determined effort was made, it was possible to destroy a bridge though casualties among the attacking aircraft would be heavy. The effect, however, of such action against so well organised a foe as the German Army was only temporary. To seize the opportunity created by the destruction of a bridge called for strong and immediate action on the part of the land forces in order to exploit and maintain the break. Otherwise only a short respite was gained and the bravery displayed by the bomber crews was rendered of little account. This was what happened at Sedan. The bridges were broken; so were the French.

Bombing Troops and Transport

Once over the Meuse, the Germans hastened to exploit their success. By 16th May the forward elements of the British Army were back on the main position on the River Dyle with the Belgians on their left, the Germans were pouring through a wide gap on the right of the 1st French Army which lay on the British right and were attacking Avesnes and Vervins more than forty miles west of the Meuse. They had now reached open country, and new targets had therefore to be attacked by our bombers. These consisted of troop concentrations, armoured vehicles and convoys of transport, which soon came to be the only targets attacked in daylight. At night railway junctions, marshalling yards and oil dumps in Western Germany and over-run Belgium were bombed repeatedly; but the German advance continued. By 19th May the enemy had reached the Oise-Aisne Canal and the famous Chemin des Dames in

the south, and to the north the line of the Scheldt held by the British Army, which had gone back to it from the Dyle. During the next three days the Germans pushed on, despite a British counter-attack near Arras on 21st May, and reached the sea at Le Touquet. Throughout these days the Advanced Air Striking Force attacked them repeatedly, inflicting heavy casualties on men and vehicles. The most successful of these operations were the bombing of tanks and motor transport near Berneuil and Puisieux on 22nd May, the attack on an enemy column blocked on the road between Abbeville and Hesdin on 25th May and the bombing and machine-gunning of another column on the Amiens-Doullens Road on 28th May.

Blenheims from England shared in these operations, working at high pressure and sustaining heavy losses. The most severe occurred on 17th May, when twelve of them were sent to attack tanks and troops near Gembloux. A few miles from the target the Blenheims, flying in two formations of six, met intense and very accurate A.A. fire. This caused them to open out, and they were then attacked by Me.109's. These shot down ten of them, one more being destroyed by fire from the ground. Not all the crews were lost. Several were picked up wounded and two returned eventually to their base in England—one from Amiens in an Anson engaged on ferry work, the other from Paris in an aircraft belonging to the regular passenger service.

An attack on 22nd May may be mentioned as an example of good planning and careful execution. The objective was the headquarters of a German mechanised division at Ribecourt. The Blenheims arrived in the owl light and, before any gun fired, they had dropped a dozen two-hundred-and-fifty-pound bombs and seventy-two forty-pounders on to the centre of the target, which was obliterated.

Two factors added to the difficulties met with by the Battles and Blenheims. Owing to lack of timely information, it was often impossible for them to be given exact targets, which meant that they had to find them for themselves. This increased the risk of casualties. There were also the civilian refugees. These streamed along, mingled with the enemy columns in unbelievable confusion. The orders were that they should not be bombed, and our pilots took great risks to avoid doing so. This living screen was of great assistance to the enemy, and he deliberately exploited it.

It is unnecessary to describe the military operations in further detail. By 29th May the Germans had penned the British Army in the area round Dixmude and Armentières while Lille, the last French stronghold in the north, fell on 31st May. The first phase of the battle ended with the lifting of the British and much of the French Northern Army from Dunkirk. The second opened on 5th June and endured until the French sued for an armistice on the 17th.

" Operation Dynamo "

An important part was played by our bombers, especially the Wellingtons, between 27th May and 4th June, while " Operation Dynamo," the code name given to the evacuation of Dunkirk, was proceeding. They laboured night after night to put down a

Low-level Attack in France. The aircraft has just bombed a German column. 1, Bomb bursts. 2, Horse-drawn transport on the road. 3, German troops running for cover into a field.

decided to continue to use it in daylight only for those operations essential for providing immediate support to the armies. All other tasks were performed at night. The result was very materially to reduce the casualty rate, though the intensity of their effort remained almost the same. During the three weeks which followed the 23rd May, the sorties of the Battle squadrons were only a fraction below what they had been in daytime. They were used at night primarily against such centres of communication as Givet, Dinant and Charleville, and also against fuel and ammunition dumps at Libramont, Florenville and elsewhere. They attacked concentrations of motorised infantry and tanks concealed in the woods of St. Gobain, Gault and in other places, as well as advanced aerodromes such as those at St. Hubert and Guise, which were used by the enemy's dive bombers. They showed themselves able to locate all these targets at night, often in very difficult conditions, and they inflicted damage which was undoubtedly appreciable.

The report of an R.A.F. officer who was captured by the Germans in France towards the end of May, and subsequently escaped, sheds light on the results achieved. " I had," he says, " *an opportunity of inspecting a railway station and marshalling yard on the Somme shortly after it had been bombed, and there is no doubt that the damage was terrific. Trucks and engines had been lifted bodily off the track, and thrown on their sides ; many of them had been set on fire, the permanent way had been torn up, railway lines buckled. . . . The general appearance was utter chaos and confusion and reminded one of H. G. Wells' film ' The Shape of Things to Come '.*"

curtain of bombs round that port, and their efforts were particularly vigorous towards the end, when the French Northern Army was being taken off. The Royal Navy were finding it very difficult to carry on in face of the enemy's heavy artillery bombardment and asked for bomber support. At short notice a considerable striking force was collected and despatched, which, according to the signal from the Admiral in charge of Operation Dynamo, carried out its work most efficiently and was a vital factor in the success achieved.

So heavy were the casualties suffered by the Advanced Air Striking Force in the early stages of the battle—they amounted to over forty per cent.—that after a few days it was

During the campaign the aerodromes of the Advanced Air Striking Force were attacked by the Luftwaffe, but never very heavily. The most serious damage was the destruction of five Battles on an aerodrome near Rheims and of six Blenheims at Vraux. They were victims of a low-flying attack, but the Lewis gunners of the ground defence shot down at least eight of the enemy aircraft and the attack was not repeated. The comparative lightness of the attacks on aerodromes is probably to be explained by the fact that the enemy's air force was mainly employed in giving close support to his advancing land armies.

It is now time to turn to the heavy bombers. Their operations were carried out entirely at night. The targets, chosen by the joint Franco-British Staff under the orders of the French High Command, were in succession, first, marshalling yards, railway junctions and trains between the Rhine and the eastern frontiers of Holland and Belgium ; then " bottle-necks " on the general line Turnhout-Namur, the crossings over the Meuse as far as Charleville ; and, finally, points of congestion behind the German armies. The weight of attack which could be put on these three main kinds of targets in any one night depended on the number of heavy bombers available, the state of the moon and the demands of the General Staffs. As the battle developed, the French called for more and more attacks on the last of these objectives. In other words, they pressed for the close and constant support of their armies in the field both by day and by night. This was at all times forthcoming.

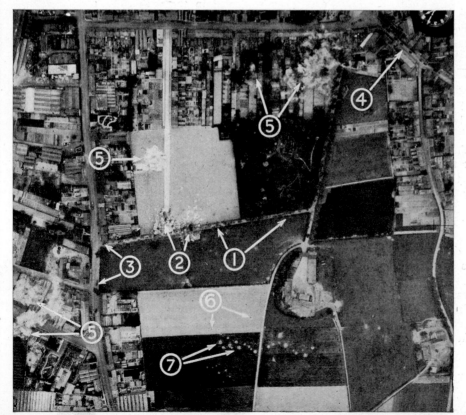

Impeding the German Advance. An attack on enemy road transport : 1, Enemy gun-limbers and transport passing through Marcke, south-west of Courtrai, and 2, Bombs bursting on and near the column. 3, Horse-drawn limbers. 4, Tank and armoured vehicles. 5, Bomb bursts and fires. 6, Small slit trenches made by the Allied forces. 7, Craters from German bombing of these positions.

R.A.F. over Dunkirk. During the evacuation, our bombers laboured night after night to put down a curtain of bombs round the port. Since the end of the campaign in France, Dunkirk has been bombed a number of times. This picture shows an oil tank burning, four others previously destroyed, and damage to the railway marshalling yard.

On the night of 20th/21st May a very large number of heavy bombers were used against roads and bridges in the neighbourhood of Cambrai and Le Cateau in an effort to interfere with the German advance against Amiens and Arras. Again, during the fighting about Roubaix and Cassel heavy forces attacked the enemy's communications in the Charleville-Courtrai-Diest triangle. Later on in June the crossings over the Somme and the Aisne were frequently attacked. It is not possible to describe all these operations in detail. They opened with the bombing by a force of Whitleys and Hampdens of the communications radiating from the important railway junction of München-Gladbach. The bombs they dropped were the first to fall on German soil with the exception of those which burst on the Island of Sylt on the night of

19th/20th March. Altogether our heavy bombers made twenty-seven major attacks on German communications, dumps, oil-storage tanks, focal points and other similar targets, between 11th May and 15th June. Among the more severe and successful were: that delivered on the night of 15th/16th May, when much damage was done to the railway junctions and marshalling yards at Aachen, Roermond, Bocholt, Wesel, München-Gladbach and Cologne, the *Autobahn* south of Duisburg, and the aerodromes at Duisburg and Eindhoven; that of 20th/21st May, when a number of bridges over the Sambre and Oise were hit, a train at Hirson derailed and an ammunition dump at Nouvion blown up; and the series of attacks delivered in the first fortnight of June on the whole length of the German communications from the marshalling yards in the Rhineland to the Somme, when particular attention was paid to Amiens, the rail head at Hirson and the junction at Aachen.

All these efforts, untiring though they were, could not save the situation. The strength of the enemy was very great. He pressed his attack with relentless determination and achieved complete success apart from his failure to trap any large part of the British army, of which 193,568 officers and men were taken off at Dunkirk, together with 123,095 French troops.

Targets of the Luftwaffe

The German air attack on France was divided into five phases. For the first three days it was directed mainly against aerodromes and landing grounds, of which eighty-one were bombed, and against railways and factories. During the second phase, which lasted till the German armies reached the Channel Ports, the principal targets were troops and transport, though the enemy was able to make fifty-nine attacks on aerodromes and thirty-seven on factories. The third phase lasted from 27th to 31st May, during which time the Germans concentrated unsuccessfully on preventing the British Army and the French Northern Army from escaping from Dunkirk. Throughout the fourth phase, from 1st to 4th June, he made raids on communications and factories near Paris, in the district of Lyons and as far away as Marseilles and other places in Southern France. In the fifth phase, which lasted until the French sued for an armistice, the Luftwaffe returned to the support of the German armies. The harm caused to the industrial life of France is difficult even now to estimate, but substantial damage was undoubtedly done to her railways and ports, though not to her aerodromes. The German attack was made without regard to casualties. By 4th June it was estimated that the enemy had lost 2,847 aircraft destroyed in the air and on the ground. This figure included about 400 troop carriers.

By 16th June it was certain that France was about to sue for an armistice. On the next day she did so. By then all our bombing forces were being withdrawn from her territory. Nothing more could be achieved by the Advanced Air Striking Force or by Bomber Command. Both had thrown themselves into the battle regardless of losses. They had dropped hundreds of tons of bombs on objectives chosen for them by the French High Command. More than a thousand tons had fallen on the railways of France and Northern Germany alone. Their casualties had been very severe. On 10th May the Advanced Air Striking Force had 135 bombers serviceable. During the next five days they lost 75 of them. From 10th May to 20th June Bomber Command lost forty per cent. of their first-line strength. The pilots and crews had done their utmost. " 'Tis not in mortals to command success." These men had done more : they had deserved it.

VII—Long Distance Attack :

THE TARGETS IN ITALY

_____

June, 1940—January, 1941

ON MONDAY, 3rd June, 1940, orders were issued for the immediate creation of a British bombing force to operate against Italy, whose entry into the war was then regarded as inevitable. The force was to be based on Salon, an aerodrome not far from Marseilles. By the 10th June, preparations on the spot were completed. On the next day, at three o'clock in the afternoon, a number of Wellingtons arrived from England. By the evening, executive orders for a raid on Milan had been received by the Commander of the Force. The necessary preparations were soon made, but he presently found himself in difficulties with the French authorities, notably with the commander of the _Zone des Opérations aériennes des Alpes._ They forbade the execution of the orders received from British Air Headquarters, maintaining that they were contrary to the desires of the French Government. The argument continued from about half-past seven until late into the night.

The British Officer Commanding was in a difficult position ; his orders were clear and were twice confirmed by telephone during the evening. Though he did not know it, they were based on decisions taken in consultation and agreement with the

French Government, which had in fact placed the aerodrome at our disposal. In view of the very definite nature of his instructions, he disregarded the protests of the French authorities and continued to make preparations to carry out the raid. About half an hour after midnight the Wellingtons were taxi-ing into position for the take-off when a number of French military lorries were suddenly driven on to the aerodrome and so dispersed as to make any take-off impossible. The French officer in charge of them informed the British Commander that he had been instructed at all costs to prevent the British bombers from taking the air. To avoid an open clash the raid was cancelled and most of the Wellingtons returned to England on the next day. While they were still in the air the French authorities called at the aerodrome to express their regrets at having been compelled to intervene in order to prevent the operation.

As the result of further instructions, the French temporarily withdrew their opposition and the raid took place on the night of 15th/16th June, the target being Genoa. The weather was very bad and only a few bombs were dropped. It was still bad on the next night, but six aircraft found and bombed their targets in Milan. This was the last bombing operation carried out from French soil. The force was evacuated from Marseilles on 18th June, the day after the French asked for an armistice. These are the relevant facts concerning its operations. They are here recorded to put an end to any misunderstanding which may still exist.

Although the Wellingtons at Salon were unable for the reasons stated to attack their Italian targets, on the night of 11th/12th June Whitleys from England succeeded in reaching Turin, where the Fiat works were bombed, and Genoa, where hits were scored on the docks and the Ansaldo works. Genoa continued to blaze with light throughout the raid. Considerable damage was done, though

this would have been greater had a larger number of our aircraft been able to reach their targets. Storms and low cloud prevented two-thirds of them from doing so. The distance they had to fly was about 1,350 miles there and back, and the Alps had to be crossed twice during the flight. Here is what the leader of the raid has to say of it :

Flares Over Turin

" *We were warned,*" he begins, " *that over Italy fighter opposition would probably be encountered. The Italian fighters—CR.42's, it was pointed out, were biplanes, with considerable powers of manœuvre and probably better suited to the task of night interception than the Me.109 or 110. We must be on the look-out for them. Nothing much happened till we were over France after refuelling in the Channel Islands. Then we ran into electrical storms of great severity. There was a good deal of lightning. When we emerged from these into a clear patch somewhere near Bourges the lightning continued. This time it was produced by French flak through which we flew till we ran into heavy weather again and began to climb in order to get over the Alps. I got my heavily laden Whitley to 17,500 feet flying blind on my instruments, but before the climb started in earnest I got a perfect ' fix ' of my position from Lac Léman. The town of Geneva at its western end showed bright with many lights. It was ten-tenths cloud over the Alps, but we knew we were crossing them because of the bumps which the aircraft felt every time it crossed a peak. Down we went through the murk till I altered course fifteen degrees to starboard so as to find the River Po. I reached it in darkness, but I could make it out by the patches of cultivation along its banks which showed a deeper shade against the prevailing black. I could not see the waters of the river. On we went till I judged we were over Turin. Then I let go a flare which lit*

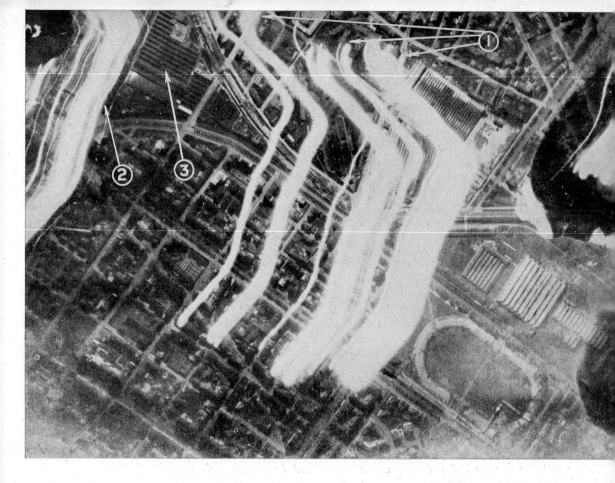

up the middle of the city. I turned back at once and climbed to 5,000 feet. When I got to that height I loosed another flare into a cloud which began to glow and shed a soft light over the whole town including the target. I ran in, dropped two bombs, one of which burst on the Fiat building, the other in the railway sidings beside it.

" The bursting of the bombs seemed to be the signal for the enemy to switch on his search-lights. These could not find us, but innumerable flashes of light, constantly renewed, appeared beneath us. It seemed as though the whole of Turin was firing at us. I have never seen anything like it before or since. But no shells could be seen bursting anywhere. We were still at 5,000 feet, but the air about us remained unlit by anything except our flare, though the flashes below winked at us with unabated zeal. I did my second run and hit the north end of the works. There was a large green flash which meant that the bombs had certainly fallen on the annealing plant. I knew that, if I hit that, the flash would be a green one. Having no more bombs I dropped more flares to guide other attacking aircraft and drew off a little to watch the show. The flares lit up everything. I climbed to 10,000 feet, keeping a smart look-out for the CR.42's. I did not see any, and no one else did ; but we did run into a heavy A.A. barrage. The shell-bursts made a squeaky, gritty noise. It was only then that I realised

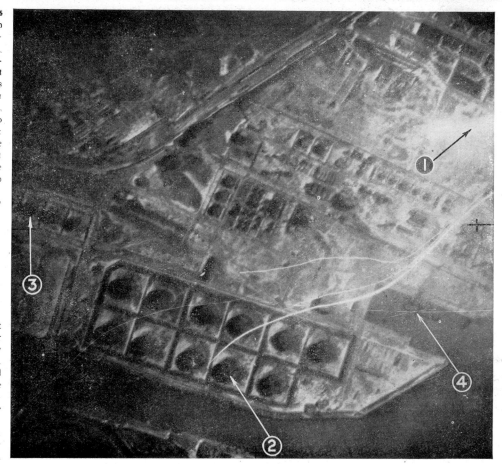

what had happened. The Italian gunners, who had been producing all those flashes I had seen below, had evidently decided that we were flying at 10,000 feet when we bombed. As we were only at 5,000, naturally we saw nothing of the bursts which were about a mile above our heads."

Valuable experience was gained as the result of this raid, and two months later on the night of 13th/14th August, thirty-two Whitleys, nearly all of which reached the target area, bombed objectives in the Plain of Lombardy. The Fiat aircraft factory at Turin was hit repeatedly, for by good chance a parachute flare fell on the roof, burning slowly and lighting up the target. Many

fires and heavy explosions were caused, both at these works and at the Caproni works in Milan. The attack was repeated on the next night, in very unfavourable weather, by four Whitleys, and a fortnight later Genoa and Alessandria were amongst the objectives bombed.

Wellington Crosses the Alps

After this there came a pause which lasted throughout September and most of October. Conditions of weather, and the constant heavy attacks which Bomber Command were called upon to make on "invasion ports," prevented further operations against Italy until the

night of 20th/21st October, when Turin
Milan, Bergamo, Savona and Aosta were
attacked. At Aosta a direct hit was scored
on the steel works. Ten days later Naples
was attacked by Wellingtons which hit oil
refineries, the railway station and an important
junction. This raid was repeated on the
night of 3rd/4th November. There were two
more raids during that month, the main
targets being the Fiat works and the Royal
Arsenal at Turin.

Three raids were made during December,
the most important being the attack on Porto
Marghera, where large stores of oil and a
refinery are situated. This was one of the
longest flights made by a bomber of the
Royal Air Force carrying bombs, not leaflets.
It took about nine and a half hours. The
aircraft took off from England soon after
six in the evening and crossed the North
Sea in darkness, for the moon had not risen.
Presently the ground beneath was seen to be
covered with snow. The temperature fell
until at 15,000 feet minus 25 degrees was
registered. About half-past nine the aircraft
began to climb and reached 15,000 feet for its
passage over the Alps. By then the night
was clear, though the moon was still not up.
Little was seen of the mountain barrier, and
when the Wellington began to descend on
the other side it became difficult to find
landmarks, for the ground was no longer
snow-covered. The navigator eventually
picked up Venice, whose towers and palaces
seemed to float upon the lagoon like one of its
own once famous fleet of galleys. The
aircraft went lower, turning in towards the
target which was on the mainland, just west
of a bridge near the docks. It was clearly
visible ; but, to make quite sure, flares were
dropped. The Wellington made a run-up
along the bridge and discharged its load of
incendiaries and high explosives which hit
the target fair and square. It remained over
the objective for some twenty minutes.
"Then," said the pilot, "we turned for home,
and as we approached the foothills of the Alps
on the way back, the navigator, who was in
the astro hatch, said it looked as if the moon
were sitting on the top of a peak . . . the Alps
seemed a little more friendly now. That may
have been due to the moon, but probably the
fact that we were on the homeward journey
had something to do with it too. Frankly, we
were none of us sorry to see the last of the
mountains."

This flight is typical of those made from
England over the Alps and back. It was not
dramatic in the accepted sense of the word.
Few long-distance bombing flights are.
Whether the aircraft has to cross long
stretches of sea or land or mountains, the
view from it is in essence the same. From
above, even the Alps lose, perhaps, some of
their dignity.

Porto Marghera was again attacked early
in January, 1941. On this occasion a thousand-
pound bomb, dropped from 700 feet, hit a
building in the middle of the refinery, causing
a large fire subsequently increased by other
bombs. The aerodrome at Padua was then
machine-gunned from 20 feet.

Moral Damage of the Raids

These were the main raids made on Italy
from this country. No account is taken of
others made from bases in the Middle East.
In number they were few and the material
damage they caused, though considerable—
large stocks of rubber in the Pirelli works
in Milan were destroyed and for some time
the Fiat works were unable to guarantee
delivery of anything—was not vital.

The moral damage, however, was undoubtedly severe. Evidence of the panic
caused in Northern Italy by the raids is
overwhelming. There is no doubt that the
population thought the entry of their country
into the war would never be more than a
gesture, which would bring some of the spoils
gained by Germany within their eager grasp.

It brought instead bombs from the Royal Air Force. The first time Turin was attacked the population rushed for the scanty, ill-constructed shelters only to find them packed with the crews of the anti-aircraft guns and searchlights appointed to conduct the defence. A number of their officers were subsequently shot for cowardice. By the end of August there was real panic in Genoa. Its poorer citizens fled daily, raid or no raid, at four in the afternoon to tunnels, where they remained until the following morning. The richer citizens of that and other towns soon had to be prevented by the police from using their cars during air raids, for they fled in such numbers as to cause serious congestion on the roads and in the country villages.

The Italians are a volatile people however, and, when our raids ceased during the month of September and the first half of October, their morale began to recover. More shelters had been built and a number of German anti-aircraft batteries installed. The public were also subjected to a much greater degree of police supervision. The raids began again towards the end of October, and once more morale became very low. By the middle of November it is clear that the Romans were suffering badly from nerves, though no bombs had fallen nearer Rome than Naples. The blackout upset them. Their shelters were very bad, especially on the Esquiline. The main shelter, the Galleria Colonna, when at last open to the public, was found to be a vast rabbit warren of mouldy sand-bags. It had to be entirely rebuilt by German engineers. Nor were Roman nerves improved by a mistake made by the anti-aircraft defences which, under the impression that a practice air raid was the real thing, opened fire with everything they had, brought down at least two Italian bombers and damaged a number of houses. Because of the frequent street accidents all motoring was forbidden after 9.30 in the evening, and the Roman press repeatedly urged both drivers and pedestrians to show greater self-control. Not only, it pointed out, were persons injured through the collisions of motor-cars or by being run over, but also by " regrettable misunderstandings which only too often end in one or both of the parties being taken to hospital."

The morale of the inhabitants of Southern Italy was for a time quite unaffected by the bombing of the northern towns. They believed that they were immune, that they were living out of range, that no bomber could reach them. The attack on Naples on 31st October came, therefore, with all the greater shock. The same symptoms of panic were immediately apparent. The inhabitants nicknamed the British pilots " milords " and could be heard imploring them not to return or, if they must, to drop their bombs into the sea. The landing of our parachute troops near Mount Vulture in Southern Italy on 10th February, 1941, added to the general disquiet. This operation was carried out by units of the army taken to their objective by Whitleys of Bomber Command. The extent of the material damage they caused is not yet known— elaborate precautions were at once taken to prevent neutral observers from approaching the area—but we do know that the moral effect was very great.

To sum up, the reason why the raids on Italy have not yet been so numerous or so heavy as those on Germany is because of the difficulties inherent in the task of bombing objectives situated so far away from the main bases of our heavy bombers. All long-distance raids depend for their success very largely on the weather. This is always an uncertain factor, especially over the Alps. They have undoubtedly had an effect out of proportion to the number of aircraft used or bombs dropped. Italian morale appears to rise and fall in direct ratio to the number of raids. At the moment it is good ; but the nights grow longer.

Mine-layer. Mechanics fixing a parachute sea-mine into position on a Hampden bomber. Great accuracy in navigation is required for the successful laying of a mine-field.

VIII—Mining the Enemy's Coast

April, 1940—Still in progress

IT HAS ALREADY been observed that towards the end of October, 1939, the Germans opened their campaign against British, allied and neutral shipping by the laying of magnetic mines, many of them dropped from aircraft. It was said at the time that this was Hitler's secret weapon of which he had obscurely boasted in a speech delivered at Danzig on 19th September, 1939. That may or may not have been true. The Germans had been making them for some years. They are undoubtedly formidable weapons, and when it became evident that the enemy intended to make the most extensive use of them we were not slow to follow suit. There was a certain time-lag. It extended from the end of October, 1939, when the enemy first planted them around our shores, to the beginning of April, 1940, when our own mine-laying campaign opened. These five months were not wasted. Mines superior to those of the enemy were manufactured, and the Hampden bomber was adapted to carry them.

After the fall of Norway, followed six weeks later by that of Holland, Belgium and France, the enemy found himself in control of some sixteen hundred miles of coast stretching from the North Cape to the western end of the Pyrenees. To supply the troops guarding the coast and the garrisons in the countries behind it is a difficult task. Much of the necessary provisions and stores must be carried by sea, and it is here that the Germans are vulnerable. They are concerned about shipping and, possessing only a small navy, much of which was destroyed during the Norwegian campaign, they cannot, as we can, run large convoys under naval protection from their supply bases to the ports in occupied territory. They seek, therefore, to send their ships creeping from harbour to harbour, hugging the coast in order to elude the vigilance of the Royal Navy and the Royal Air Force. Many of the ships are of no great size and can use the smaller ports and creeks in which to shelter and land their cargoes. There are too many of these to make the mining of all of them a feasible operation. It was, therefore, decided to mine those areas through which such ships must most frequently pass. To do so offered the best chance of interfering with enemy naval and supply vessels. Seven areas were accordingly chosen in which mines were to be laid.

Two may be disregarded for the purposes of this record, as they were allotted to Coastal Command. The five in which Bomber Command operated were : Norwegian waters, those of the Belts and the Sound to the north of Denmark, the Baltic, the Kiel Canal and the mouth of the Elbe and the Bay of Biscay. In these areas, points where mines were to be laid were chosen.

The nature of the mines used must still remain a secret. All that can be said at present is that they are cylindrical in shape, some 10 feet long, very sensitive in action and provided with a parachute to check the the speed of their fall. The mine can only be released from a low altitude, or, partially supported by its parachute attachment, it will drift through the air and not fall in the chosen spot. Great accuracy in navigation is therefore essential if the mine is to be laid where it will do most damage. The navigator takes his aircraft by the usual methods to a point on the enemy's coast near to the selected place. This is always close to land—a channel, a canal, an estuary, the mouth of a harbour. Here comes the most dangerous part of the operation. On making landfall the position of the aircraft is carefully pin-pointed. It is then necessary to descend very low and fly for so many minutes on a straight course at a certain speed. This brings the aircraft over the right spot and the mine is dropped.

It is in the accurate pin-pointing by means of landmarks on the coast and in the subsequent run up to the point chosen that the skill of the navigator is tested to the full. He must make sure of his exact position otherwise the operation is a failure. It is not unusual for a mine-laying aircraft to fly round and round and up and down for a very considerable time, occasionally even for as long as an hour, in order to make

quite sure that the mine is laid exactly in the correct place. When opposition in the form of anti-aircraft fire or night-fighters is met with, the difficulties attending such an operation are obvious. It calls for great skill and resolution. Moreover, the crew do not have the satisfaction of seeing even the partial results of their work. There is no coloured explosion, no burgeoning of fire to report on their return home. At best all they see is a splash on the surface of a darkened and inhospitable sea.

Yet the results achieved have been very considerable, especially in the number of mines sown. It is naturally difficult to say with accuracy what damage has been caused at any one moment. A mine laid in April may not claim a victim till June, July or

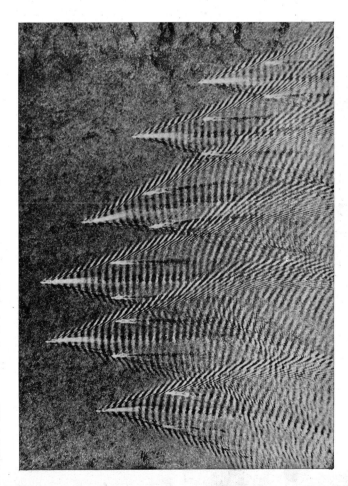

Mine-sweepers. Heavy losses, and much dislocation of sea traffic, have been sustained by the enemy as a result of our aerial mining. Here are German mine-sweepers at work ; their hulls and trailing paravanes make intricate wave-patterns on the smooth sea.

later. It is a matter largely of luck and of the volume of sea traffic passing through the area mined. Many results will not be known until after the war is over—perhaps never.

Practical Results

The following are some of the more striking losses caused to the enemy by a form of warfare in which he was the first to indulge and which has been turned against him. They can be put under two headings : specific damage, that is to say cases where a ship is known to have sunk or received injuries from a mine, and general damage when, owing to mine-laying, dislocation of traffic and delays have been caused. To take first specific damage ; in the ten months from April, 1940, to January, 1941, seventeen ships plying in the Sound and in the Great and Little Belts are known to have been sunk and eighteen damaged. There is evidence to show that eighteen more were probably sunk. These losses included a German troopship from which only 347 were saved out of a total of 3,000 on board. Bodies from this ship were being washed up on the Swedish coast through September, 1940. The main general damage caused was the intermittent dislocation of the ferry services between Denmark and Sweden and the frequent dowsing of all beacons and lightships in the area. This the Germans have forced the authorities concerned to carry out whenever any of our aircraft are about.

In Norwegian waters between May and November six ships were sunk and six damaged, the most important being a German tanker of 10,500 tons which spilt its cargo of oil over the surface of the sea. These results may be regarded as striking, since the number of mines laid off Norwegian coasts during those seven months was not large.

Difficulties of navigation in the Kiel Canal were first observed in November when ships were taking a week to sail from Bremen to the Baltic. A ship with a cargo of iron ore sank in the canal, blocking it for several weeks. The sides and bottom of the canal were damaged by another mine a little later.

In July, off Warnemünde in the Baltic, a German destroyer returning from Copenhagen was sunk with the German Commander-in-Chief of the troops in Denmark on board, and in November the German State Railways were refusing to ship goods via that port.

In August a Swedish ship sank in Kiel Bay and another in the Southern Baltic in October. In November the masts and funnels of forty-eight sunken ships were counted in the Delfzijl area.

To move to the coast of occupied France. In October a French liner struck a mine at the mouth of the Gironde and was beached. Soon afterwards a cargo boat laden with live pigs was sunk off St. Nazaire, the corpses of the pigs coming ashore in large numbers. In November an armed merchantman was sunk off Lorient.

These examples of damage taken from published sources and information which has come through other and secret channels show the measure of success achieved in the first ten months of the operations.

Apart from these specific instances of damage and loss the enemy has been forced to embark on a burdensome and continuous programme of mine-sweeping in waters which he has always regarded as entirely under his control. If the orders issued to Danish and Swedish shipyards to press on with the building of more and more ships are any guide to the situation, it would seem that he is beginning to face a shortage of tonnage. Much of this deficiency may unquestionably be attributed to the mines laid by Bomber and Coastal Commands.

The work of mine-laying goes on night after night. It has proved its worth. It has been a great military success. " Operations," as the official communiqués say, " are proceeding."

IX — Why the Invasion Armada Never Sailed

1st July, 1940—Still in progress

BY THE LAST WEEK of June, 1940, the Germans had in their possession ports, anchorages and harbours stretching from Delfzijl in the north of Holland to Bordeaux in the south-west of France. Soon after the French collapse it became obvious that there were places near these shores where the enemy might be harassed with advantage. Not only had he established himself along the western coast-line of Europe, but reconnaissance and other sources of information soon revealed that he was there preparing to deal us a mortal blow and that he was concentrating for the purpose men and material in the harbours of Norway, Holland, Belgium and France. A considerable proportion of the aircraft at the disposal of Bomber Command were immediately employed against these harbours, which soon came to be known by the general name of " invasion ports."

To have a clear idea of the very important role which they are playing, and to see how the fighting has affected them, it is necessary to examine their functions, equipment and capacity in times of peace. The invasion ports face us in a crescent. In its centre the nearest of them, Calais, is only twenty-one miles away, but all are within a distance of a hundred miles, and all were, therefore, at that time of year—August and September —within a night's sail of our coasts for the enemy's barges. The ports in the centre are mainly built to handle passenger traffic. On the flanks are some of the world's greatest cargo ports. This arrangement is admirable for the enemy's purpose. Ports built to cope with hurrying passengers can also quickly embark masses of troops, while the enormous facilities of Rotterdam, Antwerp, Le Havre and Amsterdam can ship the largest quantities of supplies in the shortest possible time. In fact, had the enemy built the ports himself for the express purpose of invading this country, he could hardly have improved on their actual layout.

To go from north to south—Amsterdam, the commercial capital of Holland, is connected with the North Sea by a canal with its entrance at Ymuiden. Here British demolition parties had done what damage they could in those few strenuous days in May when Holland was being overrun ; but after four months the Germans had made repairs sufficient for their purpose.

Rotterdam, with its outlet at the Hook of Holland, is one of the largest ports in Europe and is the natural exit of the heavy industries of the Rhine and Ruhr. It had been heavily bombed by the Germans, but the enemy had been careful only to lay low the business and residential part of the town, leaving the harbour wellnigh intact. So swift was his advance that it was possible to do very little to destroy the port's facilities.

Next comes the estuary of the Scheldt. Flushing, at the mouth, is well equipped for passengers and has extensive basins. Ghent, which is joined by a sea canal to Terneuzen on the estuary, is a commercial port of more importance than is generally realised. At the head of the navigable estuary stands Antwerp, one of the oldest and yet most modern commercial ports in the world—that same Antwerp which Napoleon said was a pistol pointed at the heart of England.

Then there is the Belgian coast, famous in the last war because of the " Wet Triangle," Bruges-Zeebrugge-Ostend. Bruges has its main outlet at Zeebrugge. The British did

3

not intend to be caught a second time, so this entrance was effectively sealed by blocking the canal mouth. The historic mole itself, however, cannot be blocked, and all through those September days German transports lay alongside the spot where the men of the " Vindictive " had fought and conquered. Ostend is the headquarters of the Belgian Marine and is admirably equipped to deal with large quantities of troops.

Next is Dunkirk. It had been heavily bombed and shelled in June. We had blocked the entrance channel as the last of our troops came away. Thus Dunkirk was of no use to the enemy's heavy ships, but some of its splendid facilities had been repaired, and the shallow draught barges could nose their way over the sunken block-ships. Everyone knows Calais, Boulogne and Dieppe, and many may have thought of the oddness of the situation when the tramp of German jackboots replaces the

hurrying feet of passengers on these well-known quays. Dieppe, however, we had time to block, and this port was of little use to the enemy.

At the mouth of the Seine Valley stands Le Havre, another of the world's great commercial ports, the home of the " Nor-mandie," and one of our main bases in the last war. Lastly comes Cherbourg, a naval base of the first importance with a splendid new harbour for handling transatlantic pas-sengers. Neither Le Havre nor Cherbourg can be blocked, and neither was damaged seriously enough to hinder the enemy.

These ports, because of their nearness to Great Britain, constituted the main threat; but in Norway, in the Baltic, in Hamburg, in Bremen, in Emden, and in the many fine ports in the Bay of Biscay, the enemy had ample facilities to launch powerful attacks on our flanks. There are, too, along the whole coast-line smaller and less important

Antwerp is a pistol pointed at the heart of England, said Napoleon. Thanks to the R.A.F., this pistol misfired for Hitler last autumn. His enormous concentration of barges, part of which is seen here in the Antwerp docks, never put to sea.

Dunkirk. If anyone doubts that Hitler had planned an invasion last September, let him study this picture. 1, Ware-house on a Dunkirk dock razed to the ground 2, Concentration of in-vasion barges. 3, Barges damaged by R.A.F. attack

ports which still had a considerable part to play.

In all these ports and harbours a formidable collection of barges and small craft were gradually concentrated. They came by devious ways. Some hugged the coast close in to shore; others chugged through the network of canals spread over Holland, Belgium and Northern France.

The word " barge " conjures up a pleasant picture of a bluff-nosed wooden craft with a gaily-painted stern supporting a cabin in which a fat and comfortable woman can be perceived while, forward, the bargee exchanges back-chat with the lock-keeper. The barges collecting against us in the invasion ports were very different. German, Dutch, Belgian and French barges are of all sizes up to 3,000 tons carrying capacity, although the largest are few in number and limited to special trades. The most common type can carry between 300 and 400 tons and if self-propelled has a speed of about eight knots.

The Germans decided to use barges for two main reasons. In the first place they were ready to hand, for they were everywhere to be found in convenient numbers. In peace time, barges carried four-fifths of the products of industry in that part of the world. There were some 18,000 registered in Holland, some 8,000 in Belgium and many thousands more in Northern Germany and Northern France. A conservative estimate made last September put the number of self-propelled barges suitable for the enemy's purpose at not less than 3,000. Those which could be towed by tugs were many times more numerous.

In the second place a barge is peculiarly suitable for the transport of vehicles which have to be landed in a hurry, perhaps in the face of hostile fire. To land a tank or an armoured car or a lorry on to a beach from an ordinary ship is extremely difficult. The vehicle must be lowered on to a lighter or pontoon, which in turn has to be run on to the beach. The barge runs direct on to it in shallow water and the vehicle can reach land dryshod by means of a ramp and a comparatively simple alteration of the barge's bows. The 3,000 barges gradually collected in ports and harbours from Amsterdam to Cherbourg had a potential carrying capacity of some 1,000,000 tons, while that of the ships amounted to about 4,000,000. They were a direct and immediate threat; but they were also a large and important target, dispersed it was true, but immobile in ports, harbours, basins and anchorages within comfortable range. No time was lost in bombing them. Ten attacks were delivered in the month of July, 1940, on barges and shipping from Rotterdam to Boulogne, as well as on barges found in the Dutch, Belgian and French canals. In September the attacks were multiplied on all these and other ports, including Antwerp, Flushing, Ostend, Dunkirk, Calais and Le Havre. They were heaviest on the two nights 8th/9th and 9th/10th September, on 11th/12th September and from 19th September to 3rd October; but they continued without much abatement to Christmas and well on into this year. They will go on as long as any threat of sea-borne invasion remains.

The ports and shipping in them being targets close at hand and not difficult to find except in very unfavourable conditions of weather can be successfully bombed by crews who, though fully trained, have not the operational experience required for targets farther afield. Even so, some of the crews are always seasoned veterans. If these targets are commonly known in the Service as the " Nursery Slopes," this does not mean that because they are relatively close to England they are therefore in the nature of things easy targets suitable for beginners. This is very far from the truth. No target is easy where the lives of the civilian population are at hazard. Nor are British aircraft

Ostend. "Go in and flatten 'em" is a phrase often heard at the briefing of crews for a raid. How thoroughly this order is carried out can be seen in the photograph of devastated warehouses on an Ostend dock.

flying over them left in peace. They are heavily defended by A.A. guns and fighters. Many gallant deeds have been performed attacking them. The most remarkable—it is a well-known story—was that of the wireless-operator air-gunner who successfully fought a fire in a Hampden which received a direct hit when over Antwerp. So severe were the flames—" the whole of the bomb compartment, with the draught coming through the large holes blown out by the projectile, turned into a sort of blow-torch "—that the aluminium floor of the air-gunner's cockpit melted in the heat. " This molten metal was blown backwards and plated in great smears on the rear bulkheads." The air-gunner, scorched but resolute, beat out the flames with his log-book. The aircraft reached base with " a hole in the fuselage large enough for a man to crawl through. . . . The rear-

gunner's cockpit and half the interior of the fuselage were charred ruins. There were holes in the wings and in the petrol tanks." The wireless-operator air-gunner received the Victoria Cross.

Up to 31st May, 1941, Delfzijl had been attacked four times, Den Helder twenty-six, Amsterdam-Ymuiden twenty-four, Rotterdam twenty-eight, Antwerp thirty-three, Flushing fifty-five, Ostend seventy-five, Dunkirk sixty-two, Calais seventy-four, Boulogne eighty-nine, Dieppe eight, Le Havre forty, Rouen once, and Cherbourg sixteen. In all 536 attacks were made. It is a formidable list and the end is not yet. Far from it. Yet, when it comes to count up the damage done, a certain prudence is necessary. Ports and harbours, though fairly easy to find and therefore to bomb, are hard to destroy. The vulnerable points are surrounded by much water and by heavy stone quays on

Bombs gone ! After a daylight attack on Berck-sur-Mer our crews reported damage to the aerodrome and an oil dump. Several sticks of bombs can be seen on their way down.

ber. It is true that there were very large concentrations of barges and other ships about that time in the Channel Ports, and that there was a considerable volume of shipping moving inland along the canals. These were heavily bombed. It seems probable that they were destined to play a part in the second stage of an attack of which the first stage was to destroy our naval and air bases and our fighter forces, and thus gain command of the air. The barges and other ships were observed to move into position at the beginning of an air attack either in order to sail at zero hour on a predetermined day or to exploit a success at short notice.

How many barges or small ships were destroyed or how many men killed or wounded in these long series of attacks is not of immediate or crucial importance. One fact stands out above all the rest. Last autumn no invasion took place. Though very great preparations were made, though invasion exercises without number were carried out for weeks along the shores of Western Europe from Arcachon to Den Helder, though small boys followed German soldiers about the streets and quaysides of Dutch ports making swimming motions with their hands and drowning noises with their throats, though the whole Continent of Europe waited breathless for the news that the twentieth-century Armada had put to sea, the German High Command made no sign and launched no attack. While we held the sea and the air, it did not dare to do so ; and as the days went by and the nights lengthened and the bombing became more and more intense, there is little doubt that the morale of the troops destined to be the passengers in the barges began to suffer. It became increasingly difficult for the enemy to use the ports for the purpose of assembling therein his invading army. The ships could not be

which bombs have a limited effect. Barges and small surface craft are very difficult to hit. To attempt to assess the damage would be a mistake. Such adjectives as " appreciable " or " considerable " can convey only a general impression, and a more accurate word may not be appropriate as long as operations are still in progress. At one time, especially in October and November, 1940, there were many rumours in America and the Continent that the invading flotillas had actually begun to put to sea, when they were overwhelmed by our bombers. The date was said to be on or about 15th Septem-

moved into position under a constant rain of bombs and in the black-out conditions which of necessity prevailed during raids. The men could not be marched on board. Our aim was to create and maintain a state of confusion. In this we certainly succeeded. To strike at the enemy in his ports before he sails against us has always been our policy. The crews of Bomber Command are following the precedent set by Sir Francis Drake, even though they are singeing the moustache of a "bloodthirsty guttersnipe," not the beard of a Spanish King.

In addition to bombing ports and harbours, occupied aerodromes and long-range gun emplacements were constantly attacked by day and night. In all, up to 31st May, 1941, there were 261 attacks made on 20 coastal aerodromes from Stavanger in Norway to Cherbourg in France. Many others inland at Merville, Amiens, St. Omer, and Abbeville, to name but four, were also included. The object was to hinder as far as possible the mounting of the mass attacks launched on this country from the beginning of August to the end of October, 1940, when the enemy finally, if tacitly, acknowledged that he had lost the Battle of Britain. Sometimes our aircraft fared ill. The attack on Aalborg aerodrome in Denmark carried out on 13th August, 1940, cost eleven out of twelve Blenheims, but on the whole our casualties in these attacks were not unduly high.

At the beginning of 1941 a new form of assault was tried by the Royal Air Force. A small number of bombers, heavily escorted by fighters, were sent out at frequent intervals by day against the enemy. The results have so far proved very satisfactory. On several occasions the Germans have been caught unprepared and have lost aircraft on the ground. Twenty-three sweeps composed of bombers and fighters were carried out between 10th January and 16th June. After that date they rapidly increased in number and strength. Thirty-six took place up to 12th July, one of the most successful being on 10th July when over 20,000 tons of enemy shipping was hit in Cherbourg and Le Havre.

Cherbourg, during the heavy raid on 10th July, when over 20,000 tons of enemy shipping was hit. Billows of oily smoke rise from a direct hit on an oil-pumping station ; to the right, a near miss on a tanker ; beyond, the quay specially built to accommodate the " Queen Mary " and " Normandie."

Flotsam. Drifting wreckage of an enemy ship, sunk by Blenheims.

X—Day Offensive in the North Sea

12th March, 1941—Still in progress

THE DIFFICULTIES and dangers of daylight bombing have already been mentioned in connection with the exploits of the Wellingtons which in the first few months of the war attacked the German Fleet on the high seas, in Wilhelmshaven and in other German naval bases. It will be remembered that during the campaign in France our Advanced Air Striking Force incurred such heavy casualties that after a few days they were used only at night except in cases of urgent need. When that campaign was over, the attack by Bomber Command on Germany was for some months entirely confined to operations during the hours of darkness. It seemed almost as though the days of daylight bombing were not only numbered but gone. The tremendous casualties suffered by the Germans during the Battle of Britain, when they attempted to operate in daylight on a large scale, lent colour to this view. It appeared to be an accepted axiom that no day bomber could live in the air against a well-organised system of fighter defence. Thus it was that, with very few exceptions, no daylight attacks took place between 15th June, 1940, and 12th March, 1941, when a new system, now emerging from its experimental stage, was first tried.

It is sometimes forgotten in this country that the North Sea is also called the German Ocean. This name has always been present in the minds of the Germans. To deny the use of that sea to us in the last war they built a powerful navy, which had to be defeated and confined to port before the German Ocean could again become the North Sea. In this war, lacking a large fleet, the Germans are seeking to achieve and maintain control over it by means of the Luftwaffe. Not the least of the boasts made in Berlin is that, thanks to the great German Air Force, German shipping has the free run of the seas from Sogne Fjord to the borders of Spain. This boast has not yet been made good, but it would be idle to pretend that the Luftwaffe is not a factor of the greatest importance in the North Sea. Under their protection German supply ships carry food and munitions of war for the German garrisons in the Norwegian fjords, in the ports and harbours of Holland, and even in the great French bases of Brest, St. Nazaire, and Lorient. The more the Germans can use the sea, the smaller grows their ever-present problem of supply. Moreover their ships do not require to venture far out from shore ; they can creep along close to land where the protection afforded by the Luftwaffe must of necessity be most effective.

During last autumn and winter, weather conditions made the problem of attacking such ships almost insoluble. With the coming of spring, however, a plan has been evolved and put into execution which is already yielding appreciable results.

How Bombers Get Through

The Luftwaffe, large though its resources are, has a very large area to defend. The coast-line of the occupied countries is about 1,600 miles in length. It is not possible for it to be in strength everywhere along the whole of that line. The defence has inevitably to be concentrated at certain of the more important or more vulnerable points. Elsewhere it is thin, and there are stretches of sea and coast where it is possible for a fast bomber to operate before the fighter defence has time to intercept it.

There are various ways in which ships or objectives on the fringe of Germany, Holland, Belgium and Northern France can be attacked, and all have been used by Blenheims of Bomber Command, to which this form of offensive action against the enemy has been entrusted.

One method is to fly over the target area by taking every advantage of cloud cover when it is available. Sometimes, when there is much cloud, bombers are enabled to travel great distances unseen. They can thus cross the enemy air defence system and press home their attacks before his fighter defence can operate. This method has been successfully used in attacking the docks at Flushing and at Ymuiden, power stations and factories at Den Helder and industrial objectives in Germany itself.

Another method is to send over bombers escorted by a number of fighter squadrons. Results have been achieved in Northern France in the area of Calais and Boulogne and farther inland. Such attacks, however, are of necessity limited by the short range of high-speed fighters.

The way in which a ship is attacked must be more closely described. Flying low, the pilot will lift the aircraft just sufficiently high to clear the mast and drop the bombs. The attack is made at full throttle, if possible from the direction of the sun. So low is the aircraft above its target that it is not usual to make any use of the bomb sight. The ship is attacked either from bow to stern or vice versa or on the beam. It depends on circumstances. The greatest judgment is needed in making low-flying attacks on shipping. In bad weather—and the weather

3ᵃ

is often bad in the North Sea—the wind-screens of the aircraft become covered with spray, making visibility almost nil. On the other hand, the ships attacked find accurate shooting with their anti-aircraft guns difficult.

The same method is used against land objectives on the fringe of the coast. For example, in April, 1941, nine Blenheims of

Attack that won the V.C. The leader of the 4th July raid on Bremen took his squadron into the heart of one of the most heavily defended cities in Germany. Flying at a very low level, beneath electric cables, he hit the target fair and square. This photograph was taken a moment before his bombs fell on the factory

Bomber Command attacked objectives on the Island of Norderney. They came in at sea level from the north in the early afternoon of a misty day, and flew in line abreast below the level of the roofs of the buildings which the front gunners machine-gunned. The aircraft pulled up over the buildings and dropped sticks of bombs on the target ; they descended once more below roof-top level and machine-gunned a flying boat and other boats in the harbour and troops drilling on a barrack square. They then broke up formation

and made out to sea, where they again went into formation immediately in order to beat off the attack of Messerschmitt 110's now roused to action. One Blenheim, a straggler, was severely handled and lost a propeller. Once, however, the Blenheims had re-formed, the Messerschmitts did not dare to close. The damaged Blenheim reached base in safety.

In another attack on an objective near Bergen a single Blenheim machine-gunned five Messerschmitt 110's on the ground and two about to take off. It dropped bombs on the runway, the second of which skidded along, pulled up under a Messerschmitt 110 and exploded. The Blenheim then joined another in the offing and the two of them, flying so close together that their wing tips overlapped, fought off three Me.110's who followed them seventy miles out to sea. Both Blenheims were hit, but reached their base in safety.

The daylight attacks on enemy ports are being extended to more distant objectives on the coast of Germany itself and some way inland. Among them are Bremen, Oldenburg and Kiel. The raid on Bremen on 4th July is especially noteworthy. It was carried out at very low level. The leader flew beneath electric power cables and in between balloon barrage cables. The target, a factory, was hit fair and square. Bits and pieces rose into the air 700 feet above his aircraft. One Blenheim came back festooned with telegraph wires. Another was last seen with its starboard engine on fire making a bombing run on the target. The leader of this attack was awarded the Victoria Cross.

A most successful attack on shipping in the harbour of Rotterdam was made on the afternoon of 16th July. A strong force of Blenheims, warmly welcomed by the Dutch as they flew over Holland in V-shaped formations, swept in to the attack mast high. They dropped their bombs among the shipping. In all, seventeen ships of an estimated tonnage of between 90,000 and 100,000 tons were put out of action either permanently or for a long time to come. Five more ships of a tonnage of 40-50,000 were severely damaged, while on shore two warehouses and a factory were hit and left burning fiercely.

In this operation four Blenheims were shot down, two of them after completing their attack.

Between 12th March and 14th July of this year, Blenheims of Bomber Command made 1,750 sorties during which they saw about 1,055 enemy ships of various classes from small warships such as destroyers, naval escort ships and flak ships down to minesweepers and fishing vessels. Of these 401 were attacked of a gross tonnage amounting to about 741,000 tons; of this total 292,940 tons was hit and sunk and a further 109,920 tons sustained minor damage due to close misses.

Another result achieved by these attacks on shipping is the imposition of a great and increasing strain on the enemy's railway systems. The railways in France, Belgium and Holland, together with those in North-Western Germany are finding it more and more difficult to cope with the traffic they have to carry. Delays are a commonplace and have become so great that the enemy is compelled to use ships more and more. The more he uses ships, the larger is the number of targets he provides for aircraft of Bomber and Coastal Commands.

All this has not been accomplished without casualties. Between 12th March and 14th July sixty-eight Blenheims have been lost in low-flying attacks.

The work is hazardous and calls for special qualities of determination.

A most successful raid on shipping in the docks at Rotterdam was carried out on 16th July. A strong force of Blenheims swept in to the attack mast high. Bomb explosions on quays and warehouses can be seen. In the distance, an aircraft is making its run-up.

XI—Battle of the Atlantic

3rd September, 1939—Still in progress

BOMBER COMMAND is playing its part in the Battle of the Atlantic. The submarine and air campaign waged by Germany against Great Britain from the moment war broke out was intensified at the beginning of 1941. The German leaders—Hitler was especially eloquent on the subject—announced that Great Britain would be starved of food and munitions by the combined efforts of the U-boat, the four-engined Kondor bomber, and the surface raider such as the " Scharnhorst," the " Gneisenau," the " Prinz Eugen " and the " Bismarck." The " Bismarck " was sunk with most of her crew on 26th May. The other three, at the moment of writing, are in harbour at Brest. The " Gneisenau " has been there since 28th March, the " Prinz Eugen " since 4th June or a day or two earlier. The " Scharnhorst " took a short trip to La Pallice and back in the last ten days of July. It is to these capital ships that the attention of Bomber Command has been directed for the last months and much of its strength has been employed to attack them in all kinds of weather.

The " Scharnhorst " was no new target. She was first found and bombed on 1st July, 1940, when she was in a floating dock at Kiel. An eye-witness account, that of the navigator in the aircraft which hit the ship with a heavy bomb, tells us what happened. " *I directed my line of sight on the floating dock,*" he said, " *which stood out sharply in the estuary. Searchlights caught us in* the dive, but we went under the beam. Then I put the captain into dive as we came on the target. The ' Scharnhorst' couldn't be missed ; she stood out so plainly . . . I could clearly see tracers coming from the pom-pom on the deck of the ' Scharnhorst '.*" After describing the damage inflicted a few seconds later on the aircraft by A.A. fire—it included a hole two foot square in the tail-plane—he goes on : " *We came down very low to make sure, and when we were dead in line I released a stick of bombs. A vast shoot of reddish-yellow flame came from the deck.*"

The " Scharnhorst " was undoubtedly damaged on that occasion, but the hurt she received was not mortal. She was out with the " Gneisenau " raiding in the Atlantic at the beginning of 1941, and both ships, after a fairly successful foray during which they sank some twenty British and Allied merchantmen, took refuge in Brest, where on the date on which this was written they still remain. One of them is in dry dock, the other alongside a quay. Both are more or less sewn to the land by camouflage netting.

They were first attacked by Bomber Command aircraft on the night of 30th/31st March, 1941. They have certainly been hit, the " Gneisenau " three times on three nights in April and again in July. There have been reports in neutral newspapers that she has been heavily damaged and that one bomb killed 128 of her crew. While no definite and final confirmation of these reports has been received, they have been very persistent. Both the " Gneisenau " and " Scharnhorst " have been attacked repeatedly, from all heights. On the night of 4th/5th April, for example, one of our aircraft, in the face of blinding searchlights and heavy anti-aircraft fire, hit the " Gneisenau " with a 1,900-lb. bomb from 1,000 feet. Another attack, from 900 feet, was made on the night of 13th/14th June. The " Scharnhorst " has been hit twice, perhaps three times, and under-water damage has also

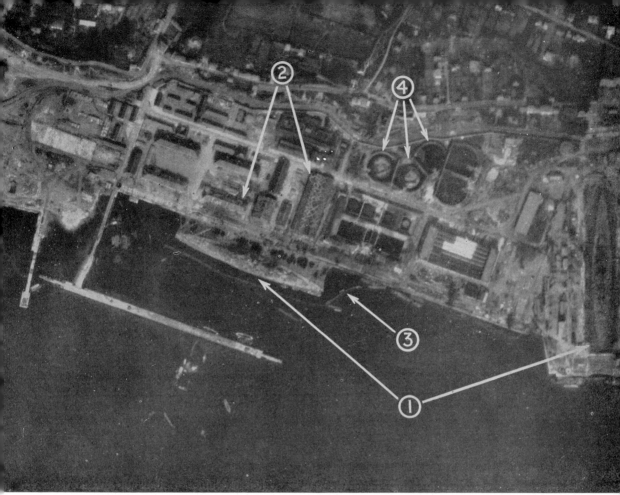

Brest. "Scharnhorst" and "Gneisenau" (nicknamed Salmon and Gluckstein by the R.A.F.) spend most of their time in dock nowadays. 1, The battle cruisers sewn to the quays by camouflage netting : stagings built at bow and stern give a square outline to the hull. 2, Camouflaged buildings. 3, Anti-torpedo boom and net. 4, Demolished oil tanks.

probably been caused to her by a torpedo attack when she was lying in the harbour. It was carried out by an aircraft of Coastal Command which never returned. The "Prinz Eugen" was hit on the night of 1st/2nd July. Serious damage was inflicted and it is believed that between forty and fifty of her crew were killed. At the moment, there is very little doubt that the "Gneisenau" has been severely damaged, the "Scharnhorst" damaged, repaired and then damaged again, and that the "Prinz Eugen" is still incapable of putting to sea.

To inflict these hurts upon the enemy warships, an enormous weight of bombs has been dropped. The great majority of them have not hit the ships, but that does not mean that they did no harm. A large number hit the docks and dockyard installations. The conditions in the port of Brest are certainly very bad, perhaps even chaotic. This has been caused entirely by the heavy bombing. The work of repairing the warships must have been very difficult, for the workmen had to work under constant air raid alarms, with no lights at all, which meant that the acetylene welding plant could only be used during the day. Many of the dockyard facilities must certainly have been broken or put out of action. Living conditions on board the ships must soon have become impossible and in all probability the crews were evacuated to places nearby, where they might be reasonably safe from bombing. This was not good for their morale.

The difficulties of an attack on Brest are not always realised. The Germans have done their utmost since it fell into their hands to make it immune from air attack. In this they have not succeeded, but an assault upon it by bomber aircraft is a hazardous operation. Brest is protected by a very heavy concentration of A.A. guns, by a balloon barrage and by a formidable array of searchlights. There are also patrols of fighters on the watch to intercept our bombers. When weather conditions are suitable a smoke screen is laid over the targets in the dock area in order to make the task of our bomb-aimers yet more difficult. It is not uncommon for a pilot to report that his aircraft has been held in a cone of searchlights for more than five minutes while he was over the target. Brest has been attacked sixty-nine times up to 10th July.

Whatever may be the amount of damage which has been inflicted on the " Scharnhorst," " Gneisenau " and " Prinz Eugen," one broad fact is patent for all to see. Not one of these three ships, vital elements as they are in the battle of the Atlantic, has taken any part in it for a long time; the " Gneisenau " and " Scharnhorst " since the end of March, the " Prinz Eugen " since the beginning of June. Hitler has been forced, during the five critical months from April to August of this year, to fight that battle without three naval units of great power which might, had they been on the high seas, have added enormously to the

shipping casualties which German submarines and aircraft have been able to cause.

Another and possibly even more important result was also achieved. There is very little doubt that by keeping the " Gneisenau " and " Scharnhorst " in port Bomber Command compelled the German Admiralty to send out the " Bismarck " in a desperate attempt to regain the initiative which it was rapidly losing. The sinking of that great warship is thus indirectly, but none the less surely, due to the part played by our bombers.

One of the most successful operations took place on 24th July in conjunction with the attack on La Pallice. Three days before, the " Scharnhorst," the " Gneisenau " and the " Prinz Eugen " were observed to be still lying in Brest. At noon on the 22nd a reconnaissance aircraft of Coastal Command reported that the " Scharnhorst " was no longer there. At 8.30 in the morning of the next day she was discovered at La Pallice, 240 miles to the south. Efforts had been made at Brest to conceal her departure by putting a tanker in the berth which she had occupied, and covering it with the same camouflage netting as had been used to hide the warship. A daylight attack on La Pallice was made by Stirlings, and the " Scharnhorst " was hit by one of them bearing " V " as its recognition letter. That night Whitleys, in conjunction with aircraft of Coastal Command, attacked La Pallice in force, starting numerous fires. On the next day a large force of Wellingtons and Hampdens with fighter escort and a small number of the American-designed and built Fortresses went in daylight to Brest, while Halifaxes attacked La Pallice, and Blenheims, with a fighter escort of Spitfires, raided Cherbourg. These attacks were carefully timed and were pressed home with great energy ; they were led by the Fortresses. The Halifaxes scored another hit on the " Scharnhorst " at La Pallice. She had now been hit at least twice in two days, and the damage done was such that she had to return to Brest, which she reached on 26th July. She was immediately put into dry dock. The Germans are at the time of writing once more at their monotonous task of repairing her.

At Brest the "Gneisenau" was hit once by the Fortresses, bombing from a height at which they were almost invisible and in-audible, and six times by the Wellingtons and Hampdens. The "Prinz Eugen" was straddled and bombs burst on the quayside and in the torpedo station.

In the course of the attacks on these three ports we lost 15 bombers and seven fighters, the losses of the enemy being 34 fighters, of which 21 were accounted for by our bombers. The anti-aircraft fire was severe. *"The black bursts over Brest looked from a distance like a huge flock of starlings,"* said the pilot of a Boeing Fortress.

These aircraft rely mainly on the height and speed which they attain, to avoid trouble. They do not fly outside the range of enemy fighters, but at the height at which they operate the manœuvring power of a fighter is greatly reduced. The Fortresses have many new devices, about which little can be said at present. The Sperry bomb sight, with which they are fitted, is an instrument of remarkable precision. A long course of training in its use is necessary—so com-plicated is it—but the bomb-aimer, once proficient, can achieve very gratifying results. Their engines are supercharged, and powerful enough to take the aircraft to a height at which without oxygen a man would be unconscious in six minutes and dead in thirty. So excellent have its design and construction proved to be, that the Fortress is habitually flown many thousands of feet higher than the operational height at which it was designed to fly. Its ceiling has not yet been accurately discovered. Rarely in the history of man has metal, stationary or moving, been taken to such heights. Great

The Enemy's Atlantic Bases.

difficulty has been caused by frosting, which at a very high altitude where the temperature is in the neighbourhood of minus 50° centigrade, covers all the windows with a thick coating of rime. A new and ingenious American device has overcome this trouble.

The crew numbers seven, two pilots, an observer-navigator, a wireless operator, a wireless operator-airgunner, and two airgunners. They wear electrically-heated clothing. To avoid breaking out into a sweat which would freeze on them and keep them cold no matter what they were wearing, they put this on in stages as the aircraft climbs. They are supplied with oxygen, of which many spare bottles are carried in special containers distributed all over the aircraft.

The effect, both physical and mental, on a man flying at the great height at which these bombers operate is, generally speaking, severe; only men who succeed in passing special tests, carried out in pressure chambers, form the crews. They run a twofold risk unknown at lower altitudes. Their bodies may become affected by the strain, and then they experience a form of cramp known as the " bends " which may immobilise them in blind and speechless pain till a lower level is reached; their minds may become subject to alternating fits of exaggerated hope or despair between which only the strongest will can strike a true balance.

Three other French ports on the western sea-board have also received attention from Bomber Command. These are St. Nazaire, attacked three times, Bordeaux attacked seven and Lorient attacked no fewer than forty-four times. Bordeaux and Lorient are very important submarine bases. Last year the attacks on them were heaviest during the month of December, but they have gone on intermittently ever since. There is no doubt that submarines have been sunk and damaged. How many in either category it is not possible to say with certainty. Two

indirect results have also been achieved. The crews of the submarines in port for a rest can no longer feel safe in their bases at Lorient or Bordeaux. The repairing of submarines has lately become far more difficult in Lorient. Taken together, these facts indicate that by March of this year Lorient had become distinctly unhealthy. The disturbance caused to rest, which to overworked crews engaged on the most perilous of duties is an absolute necessity, may well have affected their physical condition and morale.

Finally, there is the aerodrome at Merignac near Bordeaux. This is one of the main bases of the big four-engined Kondors which prey on our Atlantic shipping and which, since we have no air bases in Eire, are difficult to counter. It was attacked seven times up to 31st May, considerable damage being done on the night of 4th/5th February. On that occasion it would seem that the morale of the aerodrome personnel was affected. They all took to the woods clad in their nightshirts. Their officers took a serious view. A call for volunteers to drag the aircraft to safety was made, but produced only two candidates. Details of their costume are lacking.

The Battle of the Atlantic will assuredly be won. Throughout that grey ocean the dogged and determined courage displayed by the crews of the ships of the Royal Navy, of the reconnaissance, bomber and torpedo aircraft of Coastal Command, of the merchant vessels in convoy is slowly but surely achieving victory. The part played by Bomber Command is to harass the enemy's attacking craft, Kondors, submarines, surface raiders, in their bases not only in France but also along the northern shores of Germany in the places where they are being built. That part is being played with vigour and determination, and the success achieved is contributing in no small degree to the ultimate and certain result.

Flying over six miles high, a Boeing took this photograph during the sub-stratosphere raid on Brest of 24th July, 1941. The bombs are falling towards a target off the top left of the picture.

XII—The Mind That Plans :

OPERATIONS CONTROL

TO DESCRIBE EVERY bombing attack carried out against Germany would be to transform this narrative into a catalogue of raids. Such makes dull reading. This should be so. The most successful raids are those in which no incident occurs ; the best crew, that which takes its aircraft, unseen and deadly, to the target, bombs it and flies home again through the silence of the night. In essentials all bombing operations are the same whether the objective be Cologne, Hanover, Bremen, Berlin or any other centre of enemy industry or war production. The object is to bomb the primary target or, failing that, the secondary. In every case the bombs are carried by aircraft manned by crews who act on orders issued in accordance with a prescribed pattern, who follow the same technique learnt through long months of training, who encounter the same obstacles of wind, weather and darkness, whose success or failure is measured by the same standard.

Bomber Command of the Royal Air Force is divided into Groups. Some are first line and others are Operational Training Groups. They are connected by direct lines to Head-quarters, Bomber Command, which house the Commander-in-Chief and his staff. Of the operational Groups, some operate against the enemy at night only and some by day. During the early part of the war before bombing by night began, all the operational Groups made sorties in daylight.

Each Group is divided into stations, each station having one or more aerodromes. The types of aircraft in use vary according to the Groups.

The success of all bomber operations depends on a close collaboration of the air officers commanding the Groups and the Air Officer Commanding-in-Chief. These men are in constant touch, and though the final decision rests, of course, with the Commander-in-Chief, his subordinate commanders are allowed considerable latitude in the manner in which they carry out his orders. The commanders of the Groups keep tally of the daily strength of their Commands, which is communicated to Headquarters so that the Commander-in-Chief knows exactly how many bombers and of what type he has at his disposal at any given moment.

The close connection maintained between all those in authority in Bomber Command makes possible the operation of a flexible plan so constructed as to make any desired change quickly and with no dislocation. So carefully has the plan been worked out, so adaptable is it, that all the Commander-in-Chief has to do is to press every morning the trigger of a gun which has long before been aimed at the enemy. How he presses it, that is, how he gives the immediate orders for an attack on Germany, will be told in a moment.

The work of the Intelligence section of Bomber Command is of great importance, for it provides the Air Officer Commanding-in-Chief with the information he requires to design operations. Its staff must absorb and store facts about any subject connected with the enemy and must be prepared to place their knowledge immediately, or at the shortest notice, at his disposal. They know the Air Ministry Directives and the general bombing policy which is being pursued during any given period. They can, therefore, foretell to a certain extent what kind of information is likely to be demanded. Thus, if the enemy's ship-building yards are to be the object of attack, they will be prepared with the fullest available details about the yards at Hamburg, Bremen and other ports. If the Directive concerns oil plants or power stations or aircraft factories, they will have information ready on all these targets.

Every listed target is the subject of a separate file containing a map, photographs, plans, information on output, landmarks which enable the target to be found, notes on defences and vulnerability. Duplicate sets of these files are kept in the Operations Room at Headquarters and there is in addition a complete index of place names showing the number and nature of the targets in any town or place in Germany. The Intelligence Branch is in close and constant touch with the Plans Branch, both at Bomber Command and at the Air Ministry, with other Royal Air Force Commands, with the Admiralty through the naval liaison officer and with the Air Ministry Intelligence Service.

In the Operations Room

First, then, let us come with the Air Officer Commanding-in-Chief into his operations room at the Headquarters of Bomber Command. It is nine o'clock in the morning. Beneath a grassy mound, protected by deep layers of concrete, lies the place where he will order the forthcoming attack. Whether sunshine or rain prevail outside, inside downstairs there is always the soft light of a spring day shining steadily from half-concealed reflectors upon an oblong room of lofty and gracious proportions. It is air-conditioned, floored with rubber, and entered by a single door only. This door and the stairway leading to it are guarded by sentries and no one lacking the proper authority may pass in or out.

On the main wall opposite the door there are three blackboards each about 30 feet by 10 feet. These display the Order of Battle. The Commander-in-Chief has only to glance at them to see at once the exact strength of every Group, the whereabouts of the squadrons in it, and the total number of aircraft available.

The left-hand board is devoted to current operations. It shows what Groups are carrying out what tasks and what targets were chosen for attack on the previous night. Information upon it is written in chalk in two colours ; that inscribed in yellow shows what it was decided to do, that in red what was actually carried out. The information on the other boards is displayed in material more durable than chalk and is kept up to date once every twenty-four hours. Above these boards, which occupy the whole of one wall, is a clock, and below it the date displayed in large letters and figures. The right-hand wall of the oblong room is covered by a meteorological map showing the state of the weather. The data displayed on it are changed every eight hours. Beside it is a moon chart recording the periods of moonlight and darkness throughout the month. Opposite on the left-hand wall is a quarter-inch map of Northern Europe showing the main targets. Their positions are marked by pins with coloured labels attached to them on which the code formula for each target is written. On the back wall is a similar map displaying the main targets in Italy.

To the left of the door, a short distance out from the wall, are the desks of the controller and the duty officers. Telephones on these desks connect Headquarters with the Groups and the Air Ministry.

In the corner to the right is the desk occupied by the naval staff officer attached to Bomber Command. It is his duty to advise the Commander-in-Chief on all naval matters and to keep before him the views of the Admiralty. He is a captain in the

Nerve Centre. Beneath this grassy mound, covered with bluebells in spring, protected by deep layers of concrete, lie the Headquarters of Bomber Command.

Operations Room. The Air Officer Commanding-in-Chief, with his staff, plans the night's operations. Deep underground, the room is lofty, quiet suffused by a soft light shining from half-concealed reflectors. Its walls are lined with huge maps, charts and blackboards.

The mind that plans. The C.-in-C. at his desk in Operations Room

Air Strategy. Maps, graphs and photographic reproductions, pinned on pivoted tables, give the C.-in-C. a bird's-eye view of the whole field of battle.

Royal Navy and has two assistants, a lieutenant-commander, who is usually stationed with the Group operating against enemy shipping, and another working mostly with the Group engaged on mining. There is also an Army officer who maintains liaison with the Commander-in-Chief of the Home Forces.

In the left centre of the room stands the desk of the Commander-in-Chief. Near it are three large tables mounted on pivots so that they can be moved at will from the horizontal to the perpendicular. On the first of these are pinned the maps in current use for the night's operations. There is also a photographic mosaic of the whole territory of the Ruhr. On the second table there is a large map of Europe showing the routes to the various targets and places where German night fighters seek to intercept our bombers or where they are known to patrol. The data on this map are changed every twenty-four hours in accordance with information supplied by the Air Ministry. On this table, too, are a number of target maps grouped round a large-scale map showing where the targets they depict are situated. The third table displays graphs from which can be learnt immediately the number of times various classes of targets have been attacked. There is also a map of Berlin and enlarged photographic reproductions of the more important targets.

Targets for To-night

Seated at his desk the Commander-in-Chief makes a rapid appreciation of the situation from the reports of the previous night's operations and from information which may be supplied to him verbally by the senior air staff officer, and the group captain in charge of operations. The type of target to be attacked is already known. It has been chosen by the War Cabinet which determines the major direction of our air offensive.

Intelligence Room. Here, reports come in constantly from the Group Headquarters and Stations. Pieced together, they form the great mosaic of operations control.

The Air Ministry issues directives from time to time based on the decisions of the Cabinet. It is the duty and responsibility of the A.O.C.-in-C. to implement these general directives.

Before he can choose the targets for the night he must consult meteorological experts, for his choice is dependent on weather and visibility. These experts are civilian members of the Air Ministry and serve in all the Groups and Stations throughout the Command. Their head awaits him beside the board on which the picture of the weather is displayed. It is not always possible for the met. officer to give a final forecast of the night's weather at nine o'clock in the morning. He is, however, in a position to indicate the general trend over more than one area. The final forecast is made sometimes as late as 4 o'clock in the afternoon, after the mid-day telephone conference has taken place between the Group met. officers.

It is not unusual for the Commander-in-Chief to choose alternative areas and to issue orders for plans to be made to attack targets in all of them, for, when the weather is uncertain, he may reserve his final decision until he has obtained the final forecast. Thus, at his 9 o'clock conference he chooses a primary and a secondary target, the secondary only to be attacked if the weather over the primary should prove to be unfavourable. Only places that can be attacked by the same type of bombs as those selected for primary targets will be chosen as secondary targets, since a change-over in the type of bombs to be carried may interfere considerably with the "bombing-up" of the aircraft and lead to delays.

The met. officer delivers a short lecture on the weather, which may last some ten minutes. It is his practice to be as definite as the vagaries of his subject allow. He talks not only of the weather on the route, but of that which our aircraft will find over their aerodromes on their return.

The Commander-in-Chief returns to his

desk with his mind made up concerning the areas containing the possible targets for the night's attack. Before he chooses the actual targets he may call for information from the chief intelligence officer and the group captain in charge of operations. Photographs of different targets are brought to him. Then he makes his choice.

Having decided the target, the number of aircraft to carry out the attack is next discussed. The controller has been getting into touch with the Groups, and within a few minutes the exact numbers of aircraft available in each Group are placed before the C.-in-C., who then decides on the proportion of heavy and medium loads to be carried. Finally he discusses with the senior air staff officer the number of aircraft which can be put over any one target, during the number of hours of darkness available. This is a matter of great importance and one which

those who cry out for an overwhelming attack on a single objective are apt to forget. It is never possible to concentrate effectively more than a certain number of aircraft over any one target if the night is short.

This point decided, the C.-in-C. takes up a form marked " C.-in-C.'s Daily Allotment of Targets." On this he writes down the code formula for the targets to be attacked, the number of aircraft in each Group to take part in the operations and the proportion of incendiary and high explosive bombs to be carried. This sheet constitutes the written order for the operation. It is passed to the Controller, who at once issues the necessary orders to the Groups. The Commander-in-Chief then returns to his office. The process has taken less than an hour and in that period it is possible for him, if he so desires it, to plan the despatch to any target of any fraction or of the whole of the bomber strength available.

Group Headquarters

The scene must now be shifted to a Group Headquarters. Here, on the outskirts of some town in East Anglia, the Midlands or the North of England, the Air Officer Commanding the Group receives the orders. These are sent to him on the direct telephone line and by teleprinter. He knows the number of aircraft he is required to despatch on the night's mission, and he then decides how many squadrons he will use and what stations he will operate. Much the same procedure as that which has been followed at Headquarters, Bomber Command, is now carried out at Group Headquarters. They despatch the orders and indicate the targets to the commanders of the Stations chosen for the night's operation. The Station and Group met. officers next meet in conference over the telephone.

At Station Headquarters, the scene is still the same, but the scale is smaller. The

Air Tactics. In the Operations Room of the Station, the operation ordered by Bomber Command H.Q. is worked out in detail. What is the best route to the target ? How can it be identified ? What of the weather ?

Station commander, a group captain, sends for his squadron commander and operations officer. He repeats the orders he has received. The aiming points on the target maps are marked in readiness for the night's operation.

The squadron commander faces one main problem: How can the allotted target be most easily located and identified? This depends primarily on the conditions of visibility. Is there enough moon? In that case it should be easy. Is it a dark night with clouds? In that case the aircraft may have to spend upwards of an hour in the target area before the crew can make certain that they have found their mark. Then there is the distance between the base and the target to be considered. Sufficient petrol has to be carried for the journey out and back, and a margin provided for the time spent over the target and for the possibility that cloud or fog over the base aerodrome may make it necessary for the aircraft to be diverted to more distant aerodromes. A vital factor affecting the amount of petrol to be carried is the course to be taken. This is often not direct, since the attacking aircraft must avoid, if possible, areas where flak or searchlights have been concentrated. There is, for example, a searchlight " corridor " in Northern Germany that is well known to the Royal Air Force and has to be reckoned with every time targets at Bremen, Hamburg or in the Ruhr area are attacked.

The size of the bomb loads is laid down in the Group Operation Orders, but the load may be reduced by the Station commander if he thinks it necessary to do so for local reasons. It must be emphasised that, once the target has been chosen and the aircraft " bombed up," to change it at short notice, although not impossible, is difficult. It means changes in the fuel and bomb load. These cannot be made in a few minutes, and if the decision is left too late, it may mean that an unsuitable bomb load will be delivered at the target.

XIII—The Crew That Strikes:

NIGHT RAID

LET US NOW take a glance at the Station itself. It is in most cases of recent construction and the layout follows up-to-date principles. The buildings, camouflaged so as to cause them to blend as far as possible with the colours and contours of the surrounding country, are constructed in blocks with considerable space between them and cover a wide area. A network of roads connects them with Station Headquarters where the Operations Room is situated, with the Officers' and Sergeants' Messes, with the quarters of the men, with those of the W.A.A.F., with the hospital and decontamination centre, with the bomb dump, with the hangars, and with the airfield itself, which is surrounded by a perimeter track. For obvious reasons aircraft no longer live in hangars. They are dispersed round the field in such a way as to minimise any effects which may be caused by bombing. They remain and are serviced in the open air, only being taken to the hangars for some major repair.

It is the duty of the ground crews to keep the aircraft serviceable. Their importance is, therefore, very great. The success of the attack and the lives of the flying crew depend in the last resort on their labours. As soon as an aircraft has landed from a sortie the night staff on duty cover its engines and turrets. At daylight the ground crew, consisting of two fitters and two riggers, go over the whole aircraft from nose to tail.   The oil and fuel consumption of the engines is checked against the pilot's log.   A special watch is kept for oiled-up sparking plugs.   The wings and fuselage are checked for holes caused by anti-aircraft or machine-gun fire.   The bomb racks are examined and an electrician checks all the electrical gear, paying special attention to the bomb release gear.   The controls are tested.   The tyres pumped up.   The whole process takes from two to three hours.

In addition to the ground crews there is the personnel of the W.A.A.F.   The number of these stationed at Bomber Stations is steadily increasing.   The Women's Auxiliary Air Force carry out many of the routine duties —cyphering, orderly room work, teleprinting and telephone operating, driving, cleaning sparking plugs, and cooking.   Their work is varied and performed with great efficiency. They are rendering an essential service, often in places of great danger.   They have their own quarters and are under their own officers.

As soon as the preliminary orders for the raid have been received, the work of fuelling and " bombing-up " is put in hand.   The flight-sergeant in charge of the bomb dump and his staff make up the different bomb loads and the yellow-painted bombs are loaded on to trolley trains drawn by tractors. These trains visit each aircraft and the bombs are transferred from them to the bomb hatches.   Portable cranes are used and the bombs, which have already been fused at the bomb dump, are slung into position.   They are attached to the aircraft by means of lugs and released by an electro-magnetic system which is controlled by switches operated by the bomb-aimer.   The fitting of the bomb accurately into its rack calls for time and trouble.   The lugs attached to the bomb must be correctly aligned with the lugs in the bomb hatches, otherwise the bomb will

Bomber Station.   The camouflaged buildings are widely spaced.   The aircraft are dispersed round the field, being taken to the hangars only for some major repair.

The ground-crews keep the aircraft serviceable; every aircraft is overhauled on returning to its base.   Notice the size of this four-engined Stirling.

not fit. To do this in a hurry with bombs weighing a thousand pounds or more is not easy and requires skill, practice and team work. An expert " bombing-up " squad of twenty-eight men can load fifteen aircraft in two hours.

Briefing the Crew

Now come back to Station Headquarters. The crews, who have had a preliminary warning that they will be wanted that night, are assembled in the Briefing Room some hours before the start of the raid. They sit facing a dais behind which is a blackboard. In many such rooms the following notice will be found on one of the walls : " It is better to keep your mouth shut and let people think you're a fool than to open it and remove all doubt."

Once seated, the crews are told what they have to do that night. Here is an actual briefing for an attack on an oil target. It is the squadron commander or the intelligence officer who is speaking :—

" The target to-night is the synthetic-oil plant at Gelsenkirchen. There are two main types of oil plants in Germany : oil refineries for treating crude oil, imported or home-produced, and synthetic-oil plants. The Gelsenberg-Benzin A.-G., which is our target, consists of two atmospheric distillation units producing petrol from coal.

" The development and extension of these works was undertaken in 1938. Their output capacity is 325,000 metric tons per annum.

" The most vital section of this plant, and also the most vulnerable, is the hydrogenation plant itself—marked ' B ' on the illustration. It lies in the top half of the target running from the narrow-neck in a north-westerly direction and covers most of that part of the target. This section of the plant consists of

The Women's Auxiliary Air Force carry out many duties at a Bomber Station : a W.A.A.F. working on a pictorial map of the aerodrome.

Bombing-up is a job requiring skill, practice and team work. The bombs are loaded on to trolley trains drawn by tractors, taken out to the airfield and transferred to the aircraft's bomb hatches.

the following principal components :—

(1) Compressor house.
(2) Hydrogenation stalls.
(3) Water-gas units.
(4) C.O. conversion plant.
(5) Sulphur purification.

" A direct hit with a large bomb on the compressor house, where the low pressure hydrogen lines lead to the compressors, will cause a real explosion which is always likely to lead to severe damage in a building containing a large amount of moving machinery.

" Damage to the compressors will put the whole plant out of action, and, since they are most difficult to replace, the compressor house would be a very profitable aiming point. A hit here may cause damage out of all proportion to the size of the bomb.

" The plant lies on the northern bank of the Emscher Kanal, which at this point runs parallel and very close to the Rhein-Herne Kanal.

" The main town of Gelsenkirchen is on the south bank, but to the west of the target is an industrial residential area."

[A description of the landmarks by which the target can be found is then given and the suggested lines of approach indicated.]

" Get right up to your target and do your stuff.

" Note carefully and report the position of any outstanding landmarks for future reference, also the position of flak and search-lights. There is a strong concentration of lights reported just north of the town.

" The cameras are on aircraft, letters A, B, C, D. Get us some good pictures.

" The leaflets are on aircraft, letters Z, Y, X, W, V, U, and are to be dropped in the target area."

The approach to the target is suggested but not laid down in a hard and fast manner. Captains of bombing aircraft are allowed considerable latitude in the choice of routes to the target, once the area in which it is located has been entered. This is natural, for it is impossible to foresee the exact circumstances in which they will be called upon to make the attack.

Particulars are then given, based on the " opposition map," of what enemy defences may probably be encountered. These are of three kinds : night fighters, anti-aircraft guns (flak) and balloon barrages. The crews are shown on a map the area in which the night fighters operate, the places where they have already been encountered and the position of balloon barrages.

The navigators, who are also the bomb-aimers, are then issued with target maps. These are all that they take with them to help them identify their targets. The maps are simplified to the greatest possible degree and are printed in various colours which represent respectively woods, built-up areas, water and other easily distinguishable features. The target itself is clearly marked in red or orange. Photographs of the target are also shown to the crews and enlargements may be thrown on a screen by means of a projector.

The crews are then addressed by the signals officer who informs the wireless operators of the frequencies to be used for normal traffic, for identification and for " fixes " (signals sent out by an aircraft to enable its position to be determined by the special services established in this country for the purpose). The homing and distress procedure is also explained. The procedure connected with use of wireless is constantly changed. The tendency at the moment is for fewer and fewer calls to be made on wireless, which is coming to be used only in moments of real emergency. Navigators are expected to find their way to and from the target by other means, and the number of those who do so is increasing daily. It has come to be a point of honour with them not to ask for directional bearings, for it must always be remembered that the ideal bomber crew is the one who succeeds in going to the target and back again in the shortest possible time without being detected by the foe. Warnings, sometimes couched in solemn terms, are given against making use of the wrong procedure when in distress. Here again much depends on the training of the crew. The position of our own searchlights is explained, together with the method of obtaining their aid in case of emergency when the aircraft is nearing home.

Then the met. officer takes up the tale.

After he has finished the armaments officer delivers a short disquisition on the nature of the bombs carried and their fusing.

The briefing may last as long as three-quarters of an hour ; but usually it is shorter. The atmosphere in which it is conducted resembles nothing so much as a lecture at a university, though the attention paid by the audience would certainly flatter most lecturing dons. Everything is very matter-of-fact. There is no straining after effect. The information is imparted clearly, briefly and without embellishment. Questions are answered in the same way. The object, aimed at and achieved, is to leave no member of a crew with the excuse that he did not know that a certain procedure was to be employed or a certain course to be avoided.

After the briefing, the captains of the aircraft detailed will spend some time with their navigators working out the best course to and from the targets within the limits set. The captains will then check over the aircraft with the ground crews to make sure

After the briefing, captains and navigators work out the best course to and from the targets, within the limits set.

that everything is working. The aircraft has been previously taken off and flown round the aerodrome for about half an hour. The instruments which have to be most carefully watched are the electrical and hydraulic. A defect, for example, in the inter-communication system makes it impossible for the captain to communicate his orders to the crew and, though in other respects the aircraft may be perfectly serviceable, it is useless for operational purposes.

The navigator takes on board with him a green canvas satchel in which he keeps all his gear. It holds signal cartridges for the Very light pistol, message pads, a dimmed torch, and " flimsies " on which is typed the procedure to be adopted if the aircraft is lost and requires wireless assistance. The " flimsies " are made of rice paper, so that in the event of emergency they can be destroyed by being eaten. It is said that the taste of the ink leaves much to be desired. In another pocket a protractor, dividers, coloured pencils and a course and speed calculator are stowed ; in another, a log book, target map and a questionnaire to be filled in if the navigator in addition to dropping bombs is also going to take photographs. There is also another shorter questionnaire to be answered for the benefit of the met. officer, who is thus enabled to check what the actual weather was like during the flight and over the target and compare it with his forecast. Finally there are the Astro navigation tables. Astro navigation has been brought to a high pitch of proficiency, though it can only be used in certain types of aircraft and, of course, only when the stars are visible. Five to eight miles is the maximum margin of error if the navigator is skilful.

The crews then have a meal, after which they put on their flying clothes. These are of great variety, and are worn over their uniform. The issue of flying uniform cut to much the same pattern as the Army battledress is becoming more general. Over this a sweater may be worn and then the Irvine jacket, which contains the " Mae West." This can be inflated instantly on reaching the water. On the feet silk socks are worn and over them woollen stockings and flying boots lined with lamb's wool. The flying helmet contains the oxygen mask with a tube that can be plugged into the oxygen supply. It is not usual for the crew to wear their parachutes, but to keep them handy clipped to hooks near their stations. The pilot, however, usually sits on his. Just before leaving, the crew have each been issued with a paper bag containing the rations for the flight. These vary according to what is obtainable : the ideal ration consists of a few biscuits, an apple or an orange, a bar of chocolate, some barley sugar, chewing gum, and raisins. Each member of the crew also carries a thermos flask of hot tea or coffee. The crews are conveyed to their aircraft, dispersed round the aerodrome, in a lorry. On reaching it they get aboard the aircraft. Let us go with them.

" Gentlemen of the shade, minions of the moon."
It is dusk. The bomber crew enter their aircraft.

They go to action stations.

Though the bomber has looked huge enough on the aerodrome in its coat of dull black paint enlivened only by the code letters painted on it and by some fanciful device chosen by the squadron or by the individual captain—a bent bow with the arrow against the string, a large portrait of " Jane " of picture paper fame, a bird with spread wings, a kangaroo on a cloud—inside there is very little space. The air-gunner crawls into his turret and closes the door. The wireless operator goes to his cabin and the navigator to his, the pilot and the second pilot to their controls. If you are to walk up the fuselage, you must bend your head. There are guy ropes to hold on to.

Once at stations, the first task is for the wireless operator to check his wireless. He does this by speaking to the Watch Office. All wireless communications from the operating aircraft are received at this office, which corresponds to the control tower at a civil aerodrome. In it there is a radio receiving and transmitting set, and from that office the departure and arrival of the aircraft

are controlled. Each aircraft, in addition to the code letters showing the station to which it belongs, has its own individual letter and is known by that letter throughout the operation. The station itself has a code name. The usual way of checking the wireless is, therefore, as follows :—

" Hullo Parsnip (code name of the station), Hullo Parsnip, E for Edward calling, E for Edward calling, are you receiving me, are you receiving me ? Over to you, over."

If all is well the Watch Office will reply : " Parsnip answering E for Edward, Parsnip answering E for Edward, I am receiving you loud and clear, I am receiving you loud and clear, strength niner (nine)." It will be observed that all signals are repeated sentence by sentence to be sure that they should be properly understood.

The aircraft are sent off at short intervals of between two and five minutes. The signal to take off is made to them by those in charge of the flare path who flash a green or red light indicating whether the aircraft should, or should not, begin its run. During the periods of take-off and landing, an ambulance and a fire tender stand beside the Watch Office ready for emergencies.

On receiving the signal to take off, the pilot opens up his engines. He may keep his brakes on to lift the tail before starting the run. The Whitleys when fully loaded weigh about 16 tons and require about 1,000 yards run to take off. The Stirlings, Halifaxes and Manchesters weigh much more, but take about the same amount of run. The pilot has his wing flaps slightly lowered. As soon as the aircraft is airborne, the wheels and flaps come up. On reaching 1,000 feet, course is set for the objective. If the wind is favourable, the aircraft flies straight from the take-off on to its course. If not, it will circle the aerodrome. The captain has to make quite sure that his aircraft is setting off dead on the right course from the start ; consequently the first words spoken on the

" inter-com " are usually by the navigator. He will say : " Hullo pilot, the course is X°." As soon as the pilot has turned the aircraft on to that course, he reports : " Hullo navigator, on course." After that there is generally silence except for the navigator. He may ask the pilot questions in order to check the height and speed of the aircraft during its run to the coast.

On reaching the coast, the navigator pin-points his position and, if the aircraft is slightly off course, he gives the necessary directions to bring it dead on course again. As soon as the coast is left behind, the pilot begins to gain height and will say to the crew : " I am going up now to X feet, speed so and so." Once the course is set, the navigator is left in peace as much as possible to carry on his difficult task. As has already been said, he will work out the course by means of the stars and also by a form of wireless directional aid which can be used while keeping wireless silence.

Over the sea the bombs are made " live."

Inside the aircraft there is darkness. If the crew wish to see, they use hand torches suitably dimmed. The wireless operator has an amber light to enable him to make his entries in the log which he must keep. The captain can often be heard giving the order : " Keep your lights down."

Now come back along the fuselage to see what the rear gunner is doing. He has settled down in his seat ; his parachute is hung up behind him ; he has locked the turret doors. The turret is power-operated and swings easily in any direction. First he tests it, moving it to and fro by pressing on a pair of handles rather like bicycle handles. He loads and cocks the guns. This done he switches over his " inter-com " and reports to the captain that everything is working.

" *The striking thing about a tail turret is the sense of detachment it gives you* "—it is a rear-gunner speaking—" *You're out beyond the tail of the plane and you can see nothing at all of the aircraft unless you turn sideways. It has all the effects of being suspended in space. It sounds, perhaps, a little terrifying, but actually it is fascinating. The effect it has on me is to make me feel that I am in a different machine from the others. I hear their voices ; I know that they are there at the other end of the aircraft, but I feel remote and alone. Running my own little show, I like to sense that they are able to run theirs feeling that they needn't worry about attack from the rear. Some gunners have told me that this sense of isolation weighed heavily on them at first, but I have spent a lot of time occupied with solitary pursuits and it has never irked me, personally. . . . We must keep a good look-out, you and I, in our rear turret to-night, for, in the last month or so, the enemy fighters have been more active by night ; and quite a few of our gunners have been engaged. Previous to that we had, unfortunately, not had much opportunity of using our guns, except during the period of the fighting in France, when we got quite a lot of good ground targets at low altitudes. I remember with peculiar satisfaction a long white road in Northern France, a full moon and a German lorry column, a particularly desirable combination, if I may say so. But from a gunnery point of view our outings have often been, as Dr. Johnson said of second marriage, ' the triumph of hope over experience.' Now we are rising slowly over the familiar, darkened landmarks below. A pause, and we have crossed the coast and we ask the captain's permission to fire a burst into the sea, just to make assurance doubly sure as regards the serviceability of our guns. Out at sea, away on my beam, I suddenly see another aircraft, a twin-engined plane flying parallel to us. It is a long way off. Can it be a Messerschmitt* 110 ? *I report to the captain and keep it in view, but as it swings in I recognise the high familiar tail fin of the Wellington. Soon it has disappeared again in the darkness. ' Good hunting '.*"

Generally speaking, crews do not talk very

much over the " inter-com." They are too much occupied. Besides, they wish to conserve oxygen as much as possible. The oxygen is turned on when the aircraft has crossed the enemy's coast.

Time passes.

The aircraft is now over the Dutch coast, perhaps above a bank of clouds. If these are thick, the navigator will find his course by the stars or by the burst of flak; if the night is clear, by the water landmarks of Holland which cannot be disguised. As the aircraft draws nearer to the target, more flak becomes visible. It is of all kinds. From high up it may look like the red eyes of beasts winking from the darkness of their lairs. Then, when the shells burst close at hand, they seem like great flakes and balls of fire. In the early days strings of red balls, the old-fashioned flaming onions, which now seem out of favour with the Germans, would come up, seemingly quite slowly.

By this time the crew are keyed up, waiting for the moment when the bombs will be dropped. If the target is not easy to find, the pilot will be heard asking the navigator, who has now gone forward and is lying or sitting in the bomb-aiming position, his attitude depending on the type of aircraft, " Is it time to turn in ? " or " Is it time to make our run ? " Presently the navigator will say, " O.K., turn in." By this time the captain will have decided whether to attack direct or whether to make a gliding attack. In any case he is probably taking avoiding action—" jinking," as it is called—and is flying with engines de-synchronised.

A gliding attack tends to confuse the defences, whose sound locators cannot pick up the aircraft. When making it the pilot announces his height every 200 feet. When about to turn in for the run the pilot will

Off you go ! The pilot taxies away into the gathering darkness. A fully-loaded bomber requires about 1,000 yards run before it becomes air-borne.

"Aloft incumbent on the dusky air."

" There was a wee spot of light flak here."

say, " Opening bomb doors." This is done
hydraulically. As soon as they are open
the navigator takes charge. He brings the
aircraft on to the target by instructing the
pilot how to steer. If he wishes him to turn
to the left he will say " Left, left," repeating
the word. If, however, he wishes him to go
to the right he will say " Right " once only.
The reason for this is that there is often a
considerable amount of crackling on the
" inter-com " which makes it difficult to
distinguish the exact words spoken. If he
hears two words, the pilot knows that they
must be Left, left ; if only one word that it
must be Right, and he alters course
accordingly.

A gliding attack lasts from four to five
minutes. Presently the navigator will say
" Steady," and the pilot will then hold the
aircraft on its course until he hears the
navigator say " Bombs gone." All this time
the navigator has been gazing through the
bomb-sight. Conveniently at hand are a
number of switches by which he can control
the manner in which the bombs are dropped.
These may fall in a " close " or an " open "
stick, that is, he can either let the bombs
go simultaneously, in which case they will
fall in a bunch, or one by one at short intervals.
The bomb-sight is so constructed that it
can be automatically set to make allowance
for the ground speed of the aircraft and the
force and direction of the wind. If necessary
the bombs can be released automatically
when the aircraft has reached a certain
position indicated on the bomb-sight. They
are also released by hand by means of pressure
on a button. As soon as they have fallen
the navigator reports " Bombs gone." In a
gliding attack the pilot will continue to
glide in order to leave the target unheard, if
possible. Before he can close the bomb doors
he has to open the throttle.

It is time to go back to the air-gunner.
The temptation which besets him is to sit
still and watch the bombs dropping. This,
however, is not his job. He must be constantly on the look-out for possible enemy
fighter attack. None the less, he very often
gets a quick view, especially if the bomb is
one of the newer kind which explodes with
a large flash.

Now the aircraft has turned for home.
There are still flak and searchlights to be
encountered. The Germans appear to use
a master searchlight on which clusters of
others concentrate. Even when they find an
aircraft it does not necessarily mean that
their anti-aircraft fire will score a hit.

Wireless silence is maintained as far as
possible throughout the trip. If, however,
the navigator does not know where he is, he
may ask for a " fix." To obtain it the
wireless operator sends out a series of dots
and dashes after having given the code
letters of the aircraft. He then waits until
he receives a reply from England. The
moment their position is given, the navigator
plots a new course. If he is within a certain
distance of the English coast he can, if he
so desires, obtain a direct magnetic bearing
from his base.

Next door to the Operations Room at a

Station is the Wireless Room, where a constant watch is kept. A wireless operator is always listening in on the frequencies allotted to the Station. Once near the home aerodrome, the wireless telephone comes into play and the aircraft is brought to land by the voice from the Watch Office. A bomber pilot is trained in blind flying and in the art of landing along the Lorenz beam. A simple system of sound signals enables him to know exactly where he is, whether he can see the ground or not. The signals change as he gets nearer the aerodrome. Pilots carrying out this training, which is done with great regularity daily, are appropriately described as on the BAT flight, these letters standing for Blind Approach Training. Often in cloudy weather the pilot will ask for the barometrical pressure above the base to enable him to set his barometer and thus to know with very great accuracy what his height is above the surface of the earth.

Meanwhile the staff of the Operations Rooms at the Stations, at the Groups and at Headquarters, Bomber Command, have been waiting through the night. They plot results as they come in. These are recorded on boards in different coloured chalks or on charts by means of labels. Sometimes fog may descend on a base while the aircraft from it are still out on their sortie. Signals must then be sent, diverting them to another base where the weather is clear.

Should an aircraft be in distress, the life-saving service is warned and, if it comes down in the sea, the launches of the R.A.F. and, if necessary, the local lifeboat go at once to the rescue. The crews are provided with a rubber dinghy inflated automatically which can be shot out of the aircraft. They wear a yellow covering to their flying helmets which in daytime makes it easy to spot them from a height.

As soon as the aircraft arrives back over the aerodrome, the Watch Office sends a signal telling the captain when to land. If, as often happens, several arrive together, they are told the order in which to land and

Meanwhile, at the Station, the positions of the raiding aircraft are now being plotted.

those waiting their turn circle the aerodrome at a certain height The angle of glide indicator is set to one side of the flare path, the lights of which are switched on for each landing. They include a brightly illuminated letter " T " which is situated at the beginning of the flare path. There is also the Chance light. It is so called after the name of its inventor, not because it is turned on haphazard. It illuminates the ground at the entrance to the flare path.

When the crews have landed they are taken in lorries from the dispersal point to the Briefing Room or to the Operations Room—the procedure varies with stations— where they are interrogated by an intelligence officer who has been present at the briefing and taken part in it. To ensure a certain uniformity in the reports, intelligence officers make use of a questionnaire.

The crews are interrogated one by one as they arrive, and the interrogation is thorough, even when they report ten-tenths cloud which has made it impossible for them to see the target. Two or three intelligence officers may be employed on this if there has been a large number of crews out on the operation.

The room is soon full of pilots, navigators, wireless operators, air gunners, sipping tea or coffee and answering questions. " *I dropped the incendiaries immediately north of the dry dock . . . fires looked like a heath fire to me. . . . I couldn't see the explosions because of the searchlights. . . . Over Berlin there were so many searchlights that they lit up the ack-ack bursts . . . two rows of very vivid bright fires . . . the ' Scharnhorst ' doesn't look so ' Gneisenau ' . . . we did one of those horribly steady run-ups and I saw the bomb flashes . . . there was a wee spot of light flak here . . . when I dropped the new bomb from 12,000 feet the whole aircraft shivered as though a shell had burst near it . . . absolutely screeching round the sky . . . the moon was wizard.*"

Then, the dawn very near, they go to breakfast and so to bed.

On the control tower they await the first sign of the returning aircraft.

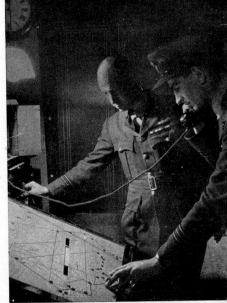

In the Control Room, officers—a plan of the lighting and runways before them—direct landing operations.

The raid is over, but the crew's task is not yet finished. Before they go to bed, they are closely interrogated by Intelligence Officers who were present at the briefing. The questioning is long, searching and exact; evidence must be conclusive before success can be claimed.

XIV—First Stage in the Knock-out :

ATTACK ON NAZI INDUSTRY

11th May, 1940—Still in progress

IT WAS ON THE NIGHT of 11th/12th May, 1940, that British bombs fell for the first time upon objectives on the mainland of Germany. Railways radiating from München-Gladbach were bombed by eighteen Whitleys. This date is of significance. It marks the beginning, modest and unassuming indeed when compared with the nightly attacks now being delivered, of that sustained assault by Bomber Command which will surely turn the scales of victory decisively in our favour.

The Germans have frequently accused us of being the first to bomb civilians. Hitler's famous patience under this form of assault became exhausted at the end of August, 1940. "We have watched these raids patiently," he said on 1st September, "and now the German bombers will answer over British towns night by night." We did not begin to bomb Germany until 11th May, 1940, two days after the Germans had dropped bombs on the mainland of this country. (They had already killed a civilian on 16th March.) These are the facts ; but the accusation becomes even more absurd when the fate of Warsaw and Rotterdam is remembered. When the chances of retaliation were nil or small the enemy did not scruple to slaughter helpless men, women and children by the thousand. The numbers killed in Warsaw and in Rotterdam were not fewer than 30,000 in each city. They have repeated these tactics at Belgrade.

There were reasons why German military and industrial targets were not attacked immediately on the outbreak of war. It should, however, be realised that the attack was practicable. We knew what the objectives were, and where they were to be found. Schemes for the destruction of vital assets in Germany had been worked out with the advice of the best experts available.

Our strategical bomber force had been designed to strike at the war industries of Germany, mainly in the Ruhr, where 75-80 per cent. of them are situated. The general plan was to use the bombers of the Royal Air Force to aid the Royal Navy in imposing and maintaining a strict blockade of Germany. His Majesty's ships and vessels were to drive German shipping from the seas and to deny all imports to the enemy. Bomber Command was to leap across the protective barrier of his armies and strike him at vital centres, so as to destroy his factories and oil refineries, and to disrupt his communications—in a word, to dislocate and bring to ruin his military economy.

The attack upon German industry upon which so much depends falls into three phases. The first lasted from 11th May to 18th June, and covered the period which ended with the Franco-German armistice. The second lasted from that date until the night of 3rd/4th December, 1940, when Düsseldorf was raided for the first time in force. The third began on that night and is still in progress with a momentum which gathers weight and speed as it goes along.

During the first phase, such of our bombers as were not employed in giving close support to the French and British armies in the field by bombing targets close behind the German lines of advance attacked communications farther back, mostly those leading from the Ruhr to Belgium and

Holland, and targets in the Ruhr itself and in Bremen and Hamburg. The first attack of importance took place on the night of 15th/16th May, when 93 heavy bombers, a considerable force for those days, bombed a large number of objectives in the Ruhr. These included railway junctions and marshalling yards, of which seven were bombed, oil plants, among them those at Duisburg, and blast furnaces at Duisburg. For the first time in this war the hot glow of fires and the jagged flashes of exploding bombs coloured the darkness which shrouded the chief industrial area of Germany. It was the beginning.

Throughout the week ending on 22nd May the attacks were continued, the oil storage plants at Hamburg and Bremen being fired on the night of 17th/18th. Some of these fires were still burning twenty-four hours later. On the next night similar damage was inflicted on the oil refineries at Misburg, near Hanover. On 21st/22nd May a small force of Hampdens scored five direct hits on trains, seven on stations, and eleven on the permanent way of railways in the West Rhineland. On the next night two more

Winged, but not crippled. After a raid on Bremen Oil Refinery on 18th May, 1940, this aircraft flew more than 500 miles back, in spite of its stripped wing—a tribute to the sturdiness of British aircraft construction.

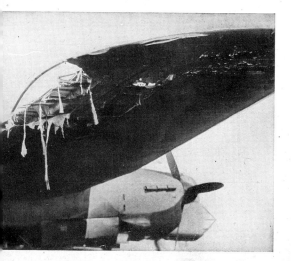

trains were hit and two blown up in the same area. Throughout the rest of May and up till 18th/19th June the same kind of targets were bombed by forces varying in size, their strength being determined by the number of heavy bombers needed to attack objectives closer to the German armies now pressing on to their victory in France. The most successful attack was that of 27th/28th May on blast furnaces and oil refineries. The programme was continued from 1st to 18th June, oil targets at Hamburg and Bremen receiving damage on two nights in the first week of that month.

In this first phase of the air attack on Germany the weight of bombs dropped was small, even when compared with that dropped during the second phase. Dislocation was caused to railway and road communications. Some stocks of oil were destroyed. Some damage was done to refineries; but the German war machine was not seriously affected. It was not thrown out of gear. It continued, at the cost of a certain increase in effort, to supply the armies of the land and air engaged on their swift subjugation of Western Europe. Much more was necessary if they were to be halted in their tracks; and they were not halted. Bomber Command lacked the strength to do so. It had neither a sufficient number of crews, nor a sufficient number of aircraft for the purpose. Even so, it did not stint its efforts. In one week from 29th May to 5th June, when the struggle was at its height, 350 sorties at night were made by heavy bombers. Light and medium bombers made 298 sorties by day and 142 by night during the same period.

The collapse of France created a situation in which Bomber Command found itself responsible almost overnight for most of such offensive operations as were possible against the enemy. Coastal Command was playing its part, but much of it had in the nature of things to be of a defensive character —the spotting of enemy submarines, the protection of convoys, the unceasing patrol of our coasts. Fighter Command was re-organising. It was shortly to overthrow the Luftwaffe in a fierce struggle soon to be known as the Battle of Britain.

Bomber Command at once addressed itself to the task of hitting the enemy in as many joints in his economic harness as it could reach. The programme of the Second Phase, which began on 18th June and ended on 5th December, 1940, was not unambitious, considering the strength that was available. Four main types of targets were chosen; aircraft factories, factories making aluminium, oil-producing plants and communications. Factories producing aircraft were obviously of immediate and growing importance as the German air attack on this country developed. A start was therefore made by bombing the Focke-Wulf aircraft works at Bremen on 22nd and 26th June, and on six nights in July. At the same time Deichshausen, where the Ju.52 is made, was bombed twice in June and three times in July, while Gotha, one of the homes of the Messerschmitt 110, and Kassel, where there are important aircraft works, were attacked seven times during those two months. Other aircraft of the same Command bombed aluminium works during June, July and August, the most important targets being those at Cologne, Rheinfelden, Bitterfeld and later on those at Lünen, Ludwigshafen and Grevenbroich.

Hitting the War Industries

These attacks were designed to reduce the strength of the German Air Force and thus to relieve the heavy pressure put on Fighter Command during that summer when the Battle of Britain was being fought. For a time it was hoped that the bombing of aluminium plants would cause such a shortage that German aircraft production would be seriously affected. As soon as France was overrun, however, Germany at once acquired stocks of bauxite which added appreciably to her supplies of the raw materials necessary to maintain her level of aluminium production. The most successful attack on an aluminium plant was that delivered at Rheinfelden on 19th August, when a large number of direct hits were scored on a new factory about to begin production. Repairs took about four months and the plant was not in production until December.

While attacking aircraft and aluminium factories, oil targets were not neglected. Here the problem was more difficult. Oil-producing plants are very well hidden in Germany. Some of them are situated in the heart of that country, too far away to be bombed during the short nights of summer. The main targets attacked during June, July, August and September last were at Gelsenkirchen, Leuna, Misburg near Hanover, Emmerich, and Pölitz near Stettin. The most successful results were those achieved at Emmerich and Misburg. The oil refineries at Emmerich were bombed on 5th July and on the 1st and 3rd August. It is known that production virtually ceased for some time. The attacks on Misburg delivered on 20th May and 19th and 27th June and the subsequent attack on 1st August, made to interfere with the work of repair, put the refinery out of commission for some considerable time, possibly for as long as six months. Damage of a more or less serious nature is known to have been inflicted at Gelsenkirchen, attacked twenty-eight times between 27th May and 2nd December, at Leuna, bombed ten times between 17th August and 19th November, and at Pölitz, raided twice in September, three times in October and once in November. With this kind of target much depends upon where the bombs fall. A well-aimed or a lucky shot may cause a breakdown, which may last for a considerable time, while a heavier attack, in which vital points escape damage, may only cause temporary dislocation.

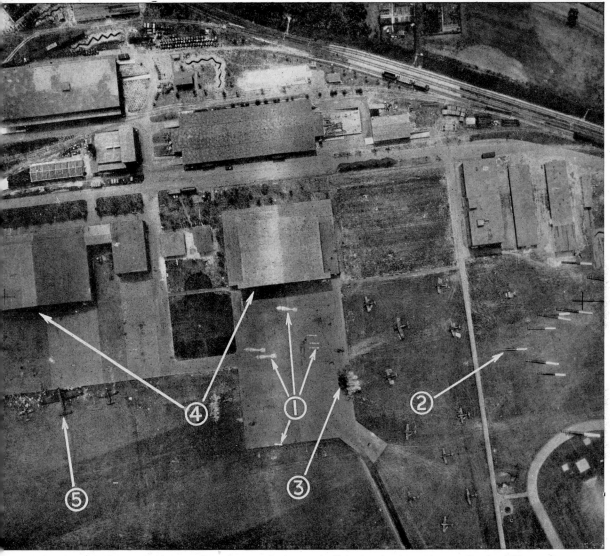

Eschwege Aerodrome, during a daylight low-level attack.   1. Bombs falling.
2. Incendiaries falling.   3. Bomb burst.   4. Hangars.   5. 3-engined Ju.52 aircraft.

Attacks on these and other industrial targets were carried out at the same time as those directed against the invasion ports. To deliver both simultaneously meant that the number of aircraft available for any particular target was limited, with a consequent limit on the damage caused. Another adverse factor was the weather, which was often unfavourable during the moon period.

At this time, too, aircraft were detached from all these targets and sent to bomb Berlin, which was attacked for the first time on the night of 26th/27th August and sustained thirty-five attacks in all before the end of the year.

The fourth class of target was the enemy's system of communications in the Ruhr and Rhineland.   This is very elaborate, and includes canals, roads and railways. To disrupt these or at any rate to cause congestion is to strike an effective blow. Of inland water transport, one target was pre-eminent—the Dortmund-Ems Canal. This waterway connects the industrial area of the Ruhr with North-Western Germany and runs into the sea at Emden. Through its placid waters moves a continuous line of barges carrying the products of heavy industry. To block it is to impose a large additional burden on railways already severely strained. Various parts of the canal, its docks and lock gates in particular, were attacked sixteen times between May and November.

Cutting the Canals

At one point it is especially vulnerable. North of Münster two aqueducts, one on four, the other on two, arches carry the canal across the River Ems. The width of each channel is only a hundred feet at water level. To destroy both aqueducts meant cutting the canal entirely, while the destruction of one would greatly reduce the volume of traffic passing through it. Several attacks were made with varying success. By 29th July it was known that the new branch had been considerably damaged. The photograph (p. 109) taken on that day shows the lock gates to be closed, a section of the canal to be dry and repair barges to be cast up on the bank. The damage can be seen at the end of the arrows numbered 5 and 6. On the night of 12th/13th August a determined attempt to blow up the aqueduct carrying the old branch of the canal was made by five Hampdens carrying a special type of explosive charge. It was a night of half moon which gave sufficient light in which to see the target. The Hampdens carefully timed their attack so as to drop the special charge at intervals of exactly two minutes, beginning at 1.30 a.m. The aqueduct was heavily

protected by anti-aircraft guns disposed so as to form a lane down which an attacking aircraft must fly, if it was to reach the target.

It was, however, decided to attack from a very low level in order to make certain that the aqueduct would be hit. One by one the Hampdens went in from the north, the moon shining in the faces of their crews and throwing the objective into relief. The first aircraft was hit and the wireless operator on board wounded ; the second was hit and destroyed. The third was set on fire but, before the aircraft became uncontrollable, the pilot succeeded in gaining enough height to enable the crew and himself to bale out. They did so and were made prisoners. The fourth Hampden was hit in three places but got back to base. The fifth and last went down the anti-aircraft lane at two hundred feet. "*After a moment,*" said the pilot, " *three big holes appeared in the starboard wing. They were firing at point-blank range. The navigator continued to direct me on to the target. I could not see it because I was blinded by the glare of the searchlights and had to keep my head below the level of the cockpit top. At last I heard the navigator say ' Bombs gone ' ; I immediately did a steep turn to the right and got away, being fired at heavily for five minutes. The carrier pigeon we carried laid an egg during the attack.*" Besides the holes in the wing, the hydraulic system was shot away so that neither flaps nor under-carriage would work. Realising this, the pilot on reaching his base flew round and round till it was light enough to see the ground and to make a landing. This he accomplished safely. He was awarded the Victoria Cross.

The second photograph shows the damage done by that Hampden. A large part of the aqueduct opposite the end of arrow No. 6 can be seen to be blown away. A new dam at the end of arrow 4 has been built to stop the flow of water.

The German railway system is com-

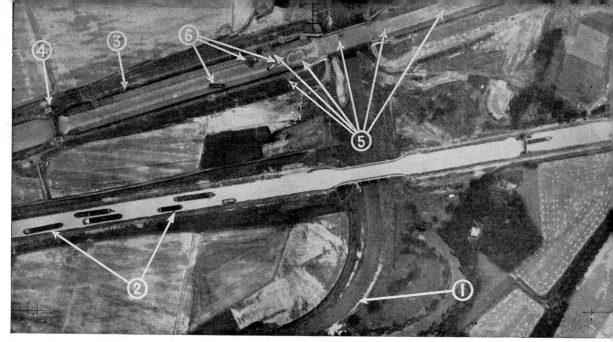

Dortmund-Ems Canal, 29th July, 1940. 1. River Ems. 2. Barges on old branch of canal. 3. New branch of canal. 4. Lock gates closed : damaged section of canal dry. 5. Craters in canal bed and hole in aqueduct. 6. Repair barges damaged and thrown on canal bank.

Dortmund-Ems Canal, 21st September, 1940. 1. New branch of canal repaired. 2. Old branch of canal out of operation : water seeping through gates at 3, and new dam built at 4 to stop flow of water. 5. Craters. 6. Old aqueduct, a large part broken away by bombing : repair work in progress. 7. Camouflage netting over the Ems River.

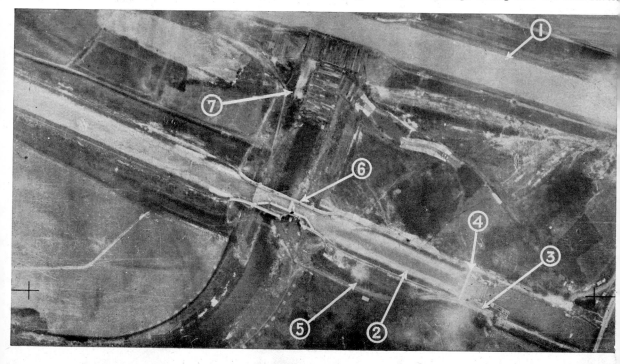

Hamm, the biggest marshalling yard in Germany, with a daily capacit
12th June, 1941. Night work, for which signal lights are essential, is gre
There is positive evidence of the widespread confusion and congestion in ge

plicated, though very efficient; but its elaboration lays it open to a successful attack. It is especially elaborate in the district of the Ruhr, which is the most important industrial area in Germany. It is there that many of her largest steel and iron works are situated. There, too, eighty-four per cent. of her coal is produced. The German railway system east of the Rhine is designed to meet the needs of the Ruhr. To handle the large number of trucks carrying the products there produced and switch them as rapidly as possible to their destination Germany relies on the marshalling yard. Of these the biggest and best is the yard at Hamm.

It stands at the north-east corner of the Ruhr and with Osnabrück, Soest and Schwerte regulates nearly all the rail traffic movement between the Ruhr and Central and Eastern Germany. Its daily capacity is 10,000 wagons. Hamm was first attacked on the night of 1st/2nd June, 1940. Between that date and 12th/13th June, 1941, it has been raided between eighty and ninety times, though a considerable number of those attacks were only on a small scale.

Marshalling yards are peculiarly sensitive to air attack, especially at night, since it is then that much sorting is done and signal lights are essential. Work must stop or be greatly reduced during a raid, and the delay upsets the traffic schedules and causes congestion. This at once reacts in all directions along the various lines leading to the yard,

ooo wagons, was raided over eighty times between 1st June, 1940, and
uced during a raid and the dislocation to traffic schedules is cumulative.
d passenger traffic which these raids have caused. Bombs are seen falling.

and the further series of congestions so
caused have in their turn similar reactions,
with the result that the dislocation is cumulative and widespread. This is what is frequently happening in Germany. Reports of
travelling difficulties are too numerous and
too circumstantial to be ignored. Ordinary
passenger trains run most erratically, and the
trials of those on board them are increased
by the regulation that trains are not to stop
in an area where an air raid alarm has been
sounded. Passengers on the platform see the
local stop-at-every-station thunder through ;
those in the train find themselves miles past
their destination. Journeys take a very long
time. Persons attending the Leipzig Fair
took five days to return from it to Portugal

instead of the normal day and a half.
Travellers from Berlin to Cologne and
Basle in October last had to change twelve
times.

One other class of target was attacked
during this phase. In September incendiary
leaves were showered on the Black, the
Thüringen and Grunewald forests and on
the wooded slopes of the Harz mountains
where military stores were believed to be
concealed. Their presence was confirmed
by numerous explosions indicating that
ammunition dumps had been set on fire.
Some of the leaves were picked up by souvenir
hunters who put them in their trousers
pockets where they burst into flame. These
snappers up of what were doubtless thought

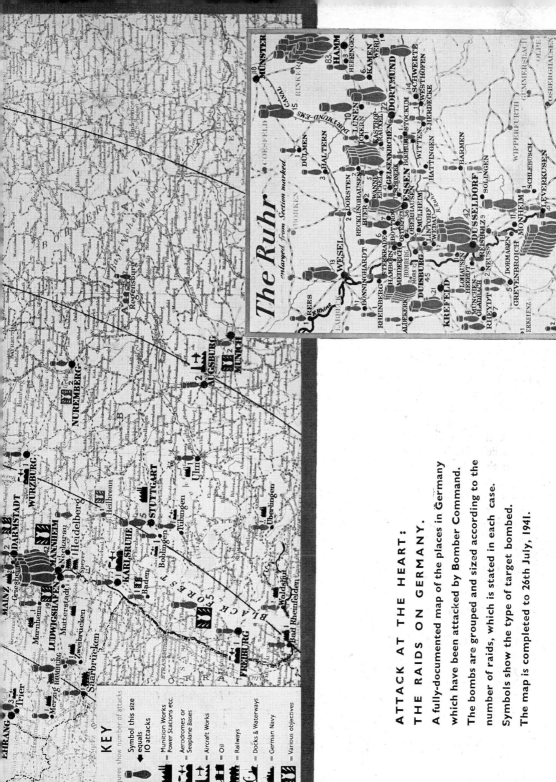

The Ruhr *enlarged from Section marked*

ATTACK AT THE HEART:
THE RAIDS ON GERMANY.

A fully-documented map of the places in Germany which have been attacked by Bomber Command. The bombs are grouped and sized according to the number of raids, which is stated in each case. Symbols show the type of target bombed. The map is completed to 26th July, 1941.

KEY

Figures show number of attacks

Symbol this size equals 10 attacks

- Munition Works Power Stations etc.
- Aerodromes or Seaplane Bases
- Aircraft Works
- Oil
- Railways
- Docks & Waterways
- German Navy
- Various objectives

to be unconsidered trifles were severely taken to task by the *Neue Frankfurter Zeitung*.

Third Phase Opens

A gradual change or rather development in our bombing attack on Germany became noticeable early in December, 1940. The weight of the attack began to be directed to special areas where industry or transport was concentrated and where in consequence the greatest amount of damage could be inflicted. This change or development was due to a very simple cause. More aircraft and more crews were coming into action. The process began shortly before Christmas and is continuing on a steadily rising scale.

The first town affected was Düsseldorf, bombed on 4th/5th December and again on 7th/8th. Next came the raid on Mannheim of 16th/17th, repeated on a smaller scale on the next night and on the night of 20th/21st. Though a larger weight of bombs has since been dropped in one night than it was possible at that time to drop in three nights, the results achieved in these attacks have been among the most successful of the bombing campaign. During the first raid on Mannheim a bomb severed the main leading from the water tower. This seriously hampered the work of the fire-fighting services. What was more important was that the marshalling yards were brought to a standstill by the failure of the water supply and of the electric current. The braking machinery in the yards is operated hydraulically, the points electrically. This meant that a wagon which normally takes eight and a half hours to pass through the yard took about seven days. When working to capacity, as they were at the time, seven thousand wagons are dealt with every twenty-four hours by the yards at Mannheim. The congestion caused by the breakdown was therefore very great. The yards at Basle, a hundred and sixty miles away, became blocked. Coal in transit from the Ruhr to Italy had to be diverted as it could not be unloaded at Mannheim. This process took so long that Italy lost 100,000 tons of coal during last winter. Traffic did not become normal once more until March, 1941.

Bremen was heavily attacked on 1st/2nd January and on 3rd/4th January, 1941, and these attacks were closely followed by the two successive raids on Wilhelmshaven on 15th and 16th January. Photographs show a close concentration of bombs on the target area, which suffered severely. Next comes the raid on Hanover of 10th/11th February, the heaviest up to that time then made in any one night. The Germans themselves, through the mouth of the city's mayor, admitted very heavy damage. Kiel has probably suffered more than any other place in Germany, though Hamburg runs it close. The heaviest raids on Kiel were on the nights of 7th/8th and 8th/9th April, when 63,600 incendiaries as well as many tons of high explosive bombs of all sizes, including an entirely new type of bomb, fell on the harbour and shipyard districts. The devastation was very great.

The attacks on Cologne, spasmodic in 1940, were intensified at the beginning of 1941. There were 24 up to 31st May, the most successful being those on 1st/2nd and 3rd/4th March. Of the raids on Berlin during this period the heaviest was on the night of 17th/18th April, 1941. On that occasion a large fire was caused by the new bomb. The first time this bomb was used was on the night of 31st March/1st April and the target was the shipyards at Emden. When it exploded, "masses of debris," said the official communiqué, "flying through the air were outlined against the glow of fires and the results appeared to be devastating." "*Houses took to the air*," said the pilot who dropped it.

Why are so many objectives in Germany attacked several nights running is a question frequently asked, especially when it is reported that the attack has been severe. The answer is : because they are so large. Marshalling yards, docks, shipbuilding yards, aircraft factories and other military objectives cover as a rule so wide an area that it is not possible to put them out of action in any one attack. In all such areas there is a large amount of space on which a bomb can fall and do no damage. The weight of bombs the Royal Air Force has been able to drop on them during any one night has not been heavy enough—so far. They have had to be dealt with piecemeal. Those who in the last war saw an artillery barrage put down on a village or a built-up area will know why. To destroy such a target completely, a shell every yard was necessary. While the modern bomb is heavier and the number needed to effect the same purpose is not, therefore, so large, it is still very large indeed. One example will suffice. The Germans had to put over an enormous force of bombers in order to obliterate a part only of Rotterdam. There are other reasons for visiting the same targets frequently. Constant bombing interferes with the work of repair and may prevent it. The workers engaged on war production are subjected to constant strain which slows down their output and encourages them to desert, if they can, an occupation become so dangerous.

By 18th June, 1941, 1,666 attacks by six aircraft or more had been made on German territory.

The attacks are increasing in severity. Between 15th June and 12th July, 1941, aircraft of Bomber Command were over Germany on twenty-six out of twenty-eight nights. They ranged the length and breadth of the industrial areas, from Kiel to Frankfurt-on-Main, from Aachen to Magdeburg. Cologne, Düsseldorf, Bremen, Wilhelmshaven, Emden, Kiel, Münster, Osnabrück, Duisburg —these names recur again and again in the communiqués.

XV—Target Area :

THE DAMAGE IN GERMANY

AT THE BEGINNING of this account it was pointed out that full and accurate knowledge of the damage caused by bombing attacks on the great variety of targets which have received the attention of Bomber Command cannot, except in rare circumstances, be obtained while the war is still being fought. Sometimes, however, a combination of factors enables a complete picture to be drawn and the whole truth, or at least a very great deal of it, to be revealed. This is not usually the case, however. The fog of war, as thick as the industrial haze which our pilots so often report over their targets in the Ruhr, wraps the results of raids in a shroud of mystery. To penetrate it much skill and patience are needed. The main sources of information about damage are photographs and reports of all kinds, from statements made in the enemy and neutral press and radio to the tales of returned travellers.

Though it is said that the camera cannot lie, it often does not reveal the whole truth. A bomb may wreak havoc in a building but make only a small hole in its roof, and this is all that appears on the photograph. The enemy has shown himself to be very skilful in covering up damage ; his repair squads are often at work almost before the " all clear " has sounded. After one attack on Bremen, last December, for example, he transformed a large block of dwelling houses, which had been demolished, into an

open square in which two days later Christmas trees were being sold. He makes great use of camouflage netting, especially over ships in docks. The " Scharnhorst " and " Gneisenau " have been festooned with it for months.

A detailed description of the work and the problems of a photographic interpreter would be out of place here ; but some of the factors which affect them can be understood by reference to the pictures on these pages. The first shows bomb damage in the centre of Aachen, where incendiaries have caused fires which have destroyed the roofs of many buildings. In such cases large-scale vertical photographs reveal what remains of the buildings as stark skeletons composed of uncovered walls and naked supports ; but the bursting of high explosive bombs in streets or in houses can create immense damage to the roadway and façade of the buildings, while leaving the roofs themselves more or less intact. The pictures on pages 120-122 compare photographs taken on the ground, showing this type of damage in two streets in Berlin, with vertical air views of these same streets. The long shadows caused by the houses in the narrow streets preclude detailed interpretation, by any but an expert, of the damage which does in fact exist ; and this should be borne in mind when inspecting the air photographs published in the Press.

Special sections of the Intelligence Services of the Air Ministry and of Bomber Command interpret the photographs taken. They are part of the body of evidence collected about each target and each raid. The Air Ministry gathers together reports from all quarters and sifts them very carefully, passing on only the most reliable to Intelligence, Bomber Command. There they are compared with the reports on the operations, to discover whether the evidence fits together and forms an intelligible pattern. The object of both

services is to provide the Air Staff and the A.O.C. in C. Bomber Command with as much information as can be collected on the damage to a particular target and on the accuracy of the bombing. They also draw up reports of damage which are sent to the squadrons engaged in attacking the enemy so that these may know from time to time, as and when reliable information becomes available, what they accomplished in a particular raid.

Every now and again in the long, continuous process of checking reports details come to light which, like the pieces of a jigsaw puzzle fallen suddenly into place, reveal something unexpected and unsuspected. In March of this year, for instance, a report was received stating that early in that month the night express from The Hague to Berlin had received a direct hit when in motion and that heavy casualties had been caused. It so happened that on one night, and on one night only, in that month, a solitary Hampden, groping its way back in thick weather from Berlin where it had failed to find its primary target, dropped its bombs on a railway junction. The time and place of this attack were, of course, given in its report. The stations through which the express had passed that night were ascertained and it was found to have been due at that particular junction at the precise moment at which the Hampden had dropped its bombs.

Again, it was learnt that on the morning of 17th March the " Bremen " had been on fire for some time and was practically burnt out. Four nights before a Hampden reported that it had dropped bombs, one of them a heavy one, on the Bremerhaven docks, but that it had been unable to observe the results. Here the evidence that it had hit the " Bremen " is not conclusive, but it is certainly very strong.

agnifying the damage, as Goebbels does it, convinces nobody. But the photo- phic interpreter must examine in the closest detail. Here, in the business tre of Aachen, is abundant evidence of widespread damage by fire and mb—" stark skeletons composed of uncovered walls and naked supports."

These examples may serve to show how the system adopted for the assessment of damage works. On the whole it may be said that it makes for conservative conclusions. The damage is under- and not over-estimated. The fact that much of the material destruction caused is not permanent and can be repaired in a period of time must ever be borne in mind. The Germans are at least our equals, possibly our superiors, in repair work. Nevertheless, it would be as absurd to conclude that the material consequences of all these raids are small as it would be to pretend that they have already had a decisive effect.

Naval Bases Hit

To come to greater detail, let us examine, in the first place, the damage done in the big seaport towns and naval bases of Germany—Kiel, Wilhelmshaven, Emden, Bremen and Hamburg. These have been attacked not only because of their intrinsic importance but also as part of the Battle of the Atlantic.

At Kiel, between 17th and 24th July, 1940, the power plant and gas works were put out of operation and two shipyards badly damaged. This damage was increased during the next month, particularly on the night of 10th/11th September. Much of this was probably repaired during the winter, but serious damage occurred in March, 1941, when in one week a large area in the Kohlen and Holstein Streets was completely gutted. Photographs taken after the heavy attack on the night of 7th/8th April reveal severe damage to the great shipbuilding yards of the Deutsche Werke, where a wide area was completely demolished. The Germania shipbuilding yard was also damaged. Much of the destruction caused in this raid was due to the new type of bomb now in increasing use. Dislocation of the public services also hampered the production of submarines.

At Wilhelmshaven three naval barracks were destroyed and many casualties caused between 29th January and 4th February, 1941. Damage in the area of the Bauhafen, in which naval workshops and stores are situated, has been severe. Many bombs have fallen on them.

Emden was the first place in Germany to receive our new bombs. On the night of 31st March/1st April, 1941, two were dropped. One fell in the east part of the town near the Post Office and Telephone Exchange, causing severe dislocation to these services. The other fell in the old part of the town, causing impressive damage. After this attack the German High Command for the first time admitted that severe damage had been done—proof enough that these new bombs were effective.

At Bremen the main damage has been in the Focke-Wulf aircraft factories, in the oil plants, and in the docks. After the raid of 11th/12th September, 1940, the fires in these burned for more than two days. By 21st January, 1941, slips at the Atlas shipbuilding yards facing No. 1 Basin had been rendered useless, and nearby storage depots had been burnt out. This caused a complete stoppage in these yards for some time. By 18th February the damage caused by raids during that month was so great that special squads of fire fighters had to be brought from Hamburg to cope with the situation. In these raids it is estimated that casualties amounted to over 1,000 killed and many thousands injured. Between 5th and 11th March the Neptune Yard, a well-known shipbuilding works, was severely damaged, and photographs taken between 25th and 31st March show much damage to all shipbuilding yards and to the main railway station. The slipways of the Vegesack shipbuilding yard, for example, where submarines are built, were so damaged that repairs were still being carried out in the middle of June. Earlier in the year the liner " Europa " was reported to be damaged, and two ships loaded with iron and steel to have received hits and been sunk.

At Hamburg also there is much devastation. The bombing of this important port began early in May, 1940, and has continued intermittently ever since. By the end of June, 1941, about half the petrol stocks had been destroyed, at least one power house put out of action, a large liner sunk, and many docks in the port rendered temporarily unusable. In June, 1940, stores of cotton and rubber in the harbour were destroyed and a naval vessel sunk, and by the middle of July the largest dry dock was unusable and the bridge over the Elbe had been badly damaged. Several gas containers had been burnt out, a number of factories and power stations suffered considerably, and sufficient damage was done to a motor works to take three months to repair. By 18th October a number of shipyards were cancelling all orders for large ships, 10,000 tons of wheat had been destroyed in three silos, and the German Press was advertising for workmen to be employed " on the re-building of Hamburg." By that date, too, a number of submarines under construction had been damaged, probably beyond repair. By the end of November many orders from neutral firms were being cancelled in view of production and transport delays. The raids on 15th and 16th November were amongst the heaviest made on the city up to that time. Several factories were destroyed, together with much war material; the railway station was hit and the Blohm and Voss shipyards badly damaged. Casualties were severe. Between 1st and 7th January, 1941, a number of direct hits by very heavy bombs were scored on the Blohm and Voss shipbuilding works, and by the end of the month a chemical factory and a margarine factory had been wrecked. At one period six submarines out of twenty-seven building had been damaged beyond repair. The raids on the nights 12th/13th and 13th/14th March caused particularly severe casualties in the districts of Altstadt and Neustadt.

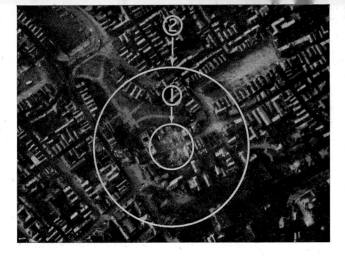

Emden. The new bomb was first used at Emden, on the night of 31st March/1st April. " Houses took to the air," said the pilot who dropped it. 1. Approximate area of complete destruction. 2. Approx. area badly damaged.

But by May the damage to the city, apart from the harbour area, was severe. The Law Courts, the Stock Exchange, the head offices of the Hamburg-American Line and the business centre of the city all bore marks of the activities of Bomber Command. It must not be forgotten that the city and port of Hamburg is one of the largest in Europe. Though the damage is impressive—only the main items are here given—there are still a large number of military and industrial targets to be destroyed.

To leave the coast of Germany and move inland: Cologne, Düsseldorf, Hanover and Mannheim have all been considerably damaged. In Cologne the damage caused by fire in the early March, 1941, raids was considerable, for the water mains were hit and the work of fire-fighting hampered. The Deutz Engineering Works suffered damage, the city's power station was burnt out and ten million marks' worth of goods destroyed in the Bonntor goods yard. In later raids the main station and the Hohenzollern Bridge, which carries all passenger traffic from the main station to the east, were hit, buildings close to the main station received some damage, the harbour area suffered heavily, and the main lines to Bonn, Aachen and Düsseldorf were damaged.

In Düsseldorf, by the end of June, 1940, a steel works had been completely destroyed, with heavy casualties, and almost a whole district had been burnt to the ground. The fires caused by the raid on the night of 15th/16th June burnt for twenty-four hours. Last winter heavy damage and casualties occurred on the night of 7th/8th December. On the night of 22nd/23rd January, 1941, the main station was hit and damaged, together with a silk factory. By the end of March the research department of one of the largest factories had been destroyed, together with a big patent food factory, a paper mill, and a large number of warehouses.

Hanover has suffered severely. The railway station was damaged early in May, 1940. By the first week in July the main motor factory stopped work for some time because of severe damage. The chief naphtha plant was also seriously damaged. By 10th February, 1941, the main passenger railway station could not be used and remained out of action for some time. The Continental Gummiwerke, Germany's largest rubber factory, a vital target, had been severely damaged. Two of the largest buildings had lost their roofs. The effect of the attacks on the Misburg oil refinery near Hanover has already been described.

Perhaps the main result achieved at Mannheim was the loss to Italy of nearly 100,000 tons of Silesian coal last winter, due to the dislocation of traffic. By the middle of September, 1940, the engineering works of Brown Boveri had temporarily stopped production, and by the end of the year the Benz motor works were ceasing to deliver products. The inland harbour—Mannheim is on the Rhine and can handle barges up to 3,000 tons—had also been heavily hit, five loaded barges sunk, and the railway so extensively damaged that trains had to be diverted. The aniline dye works were also badly knocked about. By the middle of January, 1941, a shipyard had been burnt out and 160 persons killed, seven factories had stopped work, and damage caused to the railway track which took three weeks to repair. Between 5th and 11th March the big saw mills and timber yards of the Schutte Lanz had been completely destroyed.

Münster, an important railway junction, was bombed five nights running from 6th to

Air photos may deceive.
1. The bursting of high explosive bombs may do heavy damage to roadways and façades and leave the roofs untouched. In these photographs of Schulzendorfer Strasse, Berlin, the vertical air view does not register road-level damage which the ground view of the same spot clearly shows.

10th July, 1941. It was twice set on fire from end to end and the Germans called it "the unhappy town." For once they do not appear to have exaggerated. The port area on either side of the Dortmund-Ems Canal has been destroyed, the only factory of importance wiped out, and the barracks—Münster is a garrison town—heavily damaged. The crew of a Wellington have good cause to remember one of the recent attacks on Münster. When on the way home it encountered and shot down an enemy fighter, which, however, set the bomber's starboard wing on fire. It was over the sea and the crew stood small chance of being picked up if they baled out. One of them, a sergeant, volunteered to climb out on to the wing and extinguish the flames. He climbed out of the " Astro " hatch, kicked hand- and foot-holds in the fabric and beat out the fire with an engine cover. He had a rope round his waist when out on the wing ; but had he lost his hold it would either have snapped or, helpless in the slipstream, he would have been battered against the tail fin. The Wellington reached its base safely.

One-third of the town of Aachen, bombed on 9th/10th July, 1941, is in ruins.

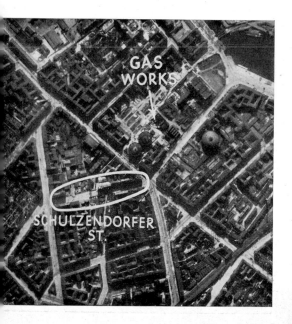

Finally, there is the damage wrought in Berlin.

In one of the earliest raids hits were scored on the Neukölln and the Alexanderplatz in the centre of Berlin, and these were followed by hits on the Lehrter and Anhalter stations and the Pariserplatz at the end of Unter-den-Linden. A number of factories were also damaged, and one near the Lehrter station burnt out. The Brandenburger Tor, that monument to the success of past aggressions, was also hit. By the end of October, 1940, the General Post Office had been gutted and the railway services between Berlin and Cologne severely disorganised. Throughout the month of November damage continued to be caused to railway stations, notably the Lehrter and the approaches to the Stettiner, and considerable damage had been done to Unter-den-Linden and a number of other famous streets. Road and tram traffic had been temporarily disorganised. By the middle of the month the Berlin underground railway system had been damaged near the Savigny Platz, and a munitions factory had closed down and evacuated to Posen. The Siemens works were hit in several raids. The heavy damage caused to these works, which employ thousands of workers, was one of the main topics of conversation in Berlin at that time. Before Christmas heavy damage was caused in the Weissensee district and also to power stations. In the last week of the year the arsenal in the Friedrichsplatz was blown up, and the old Royal Palace hit.

Bombs had also fallen along that superb example of Prussian bad taste, the Sieges Allee. The law courts had been hit and the windows of the Home Office broken. In January, 1941, barracks at Charlottenburg, a suburb of Berlin, were completely destroyed. In February a big departmental store in the Alexanderplatz was burnt out, and the Siemens factory once more damaged. The raid on the night of 12th/13th March was particularly effective, a goods station suffering severely, S.S. barracks in the Grosslichtenfeld being destroyed, and a chemical factory damaged beyond repair.

In April the Unter-den-Linden district, in the heart of Berlin, was severely damaged. It is known that the Opera House, the War Museum (which contained the death mask of Hindenburg), and the old Royal Stables were hit. People living near the Witzleben station will remember the first of our new bombs to be dropped on Berlin. In an area about 500 yards in diameter it blew out all windows and removed the tiles from all the roofs.

Though in their preparations for war the Nazi leaders did not forget air-raid precautions, the plans drawn up as far back as 1934 have proved inadequate when put to the test. There are shelters in every block of flats, but the experts appear to have miscalculated the penetrating power of a heavy bomb. Deep shelters away from buildings and water mains are now being hastily constructed.

Much more damage has been done to Germany than that which has been briefly outlined. Much more will be done before the war is over.

German Home Morale

So much for material damage. What, however, has been the effect of our raids on the morale of the Germans? The importance of this aspect of our bombing attacks on them needs no emphasis. As soon as German morale begins to wilt, victory will be in sight.

The effects of raids on civilian morale is very hard to assess. It is easy to fall into the one or the other pitfall—over-optimism or over-pessimism. One thing is certain. As yet no final result has been achieved. There are no outward signs of any break in morale, and it would be rash to prophesy the moment at which they will appear.

Air photos may deceive.—2. Invalide Strasse, Berlin, shows no sign of damage from above, except to the experienced interprete The long shadows caused by the house hide effects of R.A.F. bombing which ar noticeable enough from the street-leve

INVALIDEN
ST.
STETTINER STATION

Certain general tendencies, however, have been observed and can be set down. Their appearance and duration correspond roughly to the three phases of our attacks, of which the third is now in full development. During the first phase there was undoubtedly considerable fear amounting almost to panic in each town visited by the aircraft of Bomber Command. This gradually gave way, during the second phase, to annoyance at the general disturbance and discomfort suffered. The third and present phase, in which our attacks have assumed a more concentrated form, is producing a feeling of nervousness and apprehension at the increasing weight of the assault.

In the beginning the Germans behaved very much as we did when they first began to bomb us. It will be remembered that during that early period trains slowed down to fifteen miles an hour ; buses stopped at the kerbside ; most persons in business or Government offices or in the open streets went to shelters. With us this phase did not last long ; in Germany it did. At first sight this is surprising, when the weight of our attack is compared with the weight of theirs. It must, however, be remembered that the Germans had been promised by Göring complete immunity from bombing attacks No enemy aircraft, he had said, could live long in the air above German soil. When this proved to be false, the shock was all the greater. Göring's confidence in the power of the Luftwaffe and the German A.A. defences to keep the British bomber out of Germany seems to have been shared by other and less exalted authorities. Little or no provision had been made to evacuate children from the towns, and the number and quality of the shelters were very inadequate. Fortunately for the Germans the first attacks began in May, 1940, and they had, therefore, all the months of the summer with their long days and short nights in which to become accustomed to air raids.

The psychology of the German population during the second phase, when we were bombing selected targets comparatively small in size, may be compared with our own during the same period. After the first shock the people of London, Coventry and the other towns of Great Britain entered upon a mood of stubborn fortitude and stoical determination. The Germans found courage and the strength to endure from observing the nature of our attacks. Many a tribute was soon paid to the accuracy of our bombing. It was said on all sides—the reports are numerous and too circumstantial to be ignored—that the British only attacked military objectives and that anyone not living in their neighbourhood was in no danger. During the summer and autumn months of 1940, for example, the population of Hamburg so recovered their morale that, knowing our objectives were in the harbour area, some of them with the connivance of their wardens were in the habit of watching the raids from afar off.

In September, 1940, the regularity with which we flew over the Ruhr had one unforeseen effect. For some time our bombers regularly passed over that industrial district at the moment when the change-over to the night shift was taking place. All forms of transport at once came to a halt. The workers leaving the factories could not go home. Those due to start their work could not get there to do so. This state of affairs endured until the shift hours were altered. The night shift arrived on duty one hour earlier so as to make certain that they would be at work before the sirens wailed.

Between September and December, the shelter reconstruction programme that was being undertaken had not proceeded far, and with the increasing cold weather the inadequacy and discomfort of the shelters had a lowering effect on morale.

The third phase of our attack, which has lasted since the beginning of December, 1940, has quite clearly created a feeling of nervousness and apprehension among the populations of the large industrial centres of Germany. For a long time the German general public have been taught to believe in the great superiority of the Luftwaffe over the Royal Air Force, both in men and aircraft. This belief is still deeply rooted, and the ordinary German citizen is under the impression that the increased weight of our attack is due not to the expansion of the Royal Air Force, but to the numbers of American aircraft and heavy bombs which that Force is said to be using.

Morale took a downward curve after the heavy raids on Kiel on the nights of 7th/8th and 8th/9th April, 1941. Complaints began to be made about the inadequacy of the A.R.P. and fire-fighting services. A feeling of depression spread abroad over Hamburg and the citizens are still under its influence. After the second of the two heavy raids in March last which took place on the nights of 12th/13th and 13th/14th, the main railway station had to be closed, for the numbers trying to leave the city were becoming out of control.

To enumerate those places in Germany where morale is at its best or at its worst is very difficult, for the simple reason that the temper of the people rises and falls like the temperature of a fever patient. Probably the citizens of Bremen, Hamburg and Kiel show the lowest morale at this moment, while many reports describe how irritable the population of Berlin becomes through lack of sleep, even though the attack is not on a heavy scale.

To sum up—that German morale has suffered is without question, that it will go on to suffer is quite certain, that it is fast cracking under the strain is, however, not yet true. What the future holds no one can foretell. But it must not be forgotten that the attacks delivered by Bomber Command are steadily increasing in weight and severity.

XVI—One Thing is Certain

THE STORY of Bomber Command has been told in brief up to July, 1941. There, for the moment, it must end, at a point in time when in reality it has only just begun. We can look with confidence to the prospect before us, to the Stirlings, the Halifaxes, the Manchesters, the Fortresses and the rest, of which there are great expectations. These aircraft are to deliver that overwhelming onslaught which will bring the enemy to his knees and then lay him prostrate in the dust of his own ruined cities. When that day comes, as come it will, the Battles and Blenheims, the Whitleys, the Wellingtons and the Hampdens must not be forgotten. It is the purpose of this record to keep them in mind. They have carried the weight of our bombing attacks for the first year and a half of war, and they are still playing a very important part. They have proved themselves to be stout aircraft stoutly flown by a force which, beginning as a sturdy adolescent, is now on the threshold of manhood.

Its history is the story of a force built up slowly from sound principles resolutely applied. Let there be no mistake. The policy of the Royal Air Force is a long-term policy. Long before this war began, those in authority, when faced with the rapidly growing numbers of the Luftwaffe, decided that to seek parity in mere numbers, even if this could be done quickly, was wrong and dangerous. It was a short cut not to victory

"Their hearts are high."

but to defeat. That is why our bombers were built to fly long distances with heavy loads in almost any kind of weather. That is why they were given a heavy defensive armament. That is why their crews were trained to be self-sufficient, to rely on their own skill to get them to the target and back again, to take, as it were, their operations room, where all the thinking and planning is done, into the aircraft with them.

The decision to concentrate on quality, not quantity, was bold, but who shall say that it was wrong? It meant that for long months this country had a bombing force very inferior in numbers to that of the enemy. It meant that during that time the blows it could strike, though persistently and scientifically delivered, could not have the weight of those dealt by the enemy. But it meant, too, that once the industries of Great Britain and America got into their full stride, once the huge air training schemes developing in Canada, Australia, South Africa and else-

where began to produce results, nothing could prevent the achievement of air supremacy and therefore of victory.

That day is approaching. This is not a boast nor a vain prophecy. The figures for the weight of high explosive and incendiary bombs dropped on Germany, on German shipping, on German-occupied territory are proof that this is so. The weight of bombs dropped during May, 1941, was more than twice the weight dropped in May, 1940, when the attacks by Bomber Command began, and the weight of bombs dropped in June, 1941, was half as much again as that of the bombs dropped in the previous month. During June, 1941, more than three and a half times the weight of bombs were falling on the enemy than fell at the beginning of the bombing campaign. What this means can be best understood if it is realised that during June this year more bombs fell on Germany than were dropped on the British Isles during April of this year, which is

claimed by the Germans to be their record month for 1941.

The figures of bombs dropped show a fairly constant rate for the summer months of 1940, rising momentarily in September by as much as eighty-four per cent., when the invasion ports were fiercely attacked, and falling through the winter months, when bad weather reduced the number of sorties, to a figure for January, 1941, below that of May, 1940. After that month the rise is steady and, since April, sharp. The daily average increase for that month as compared with the daily average of bombs dropped during all the winter months from 1st October, 1940, to 31st March, 1941, was 105 per cent. It is not necessary to add more to show the results which this policy is now producing.

It is a policy well in keeping with our national character. Blended in it are courage and caution and a full measure of that spirit of determination usually described as " dogged does it." Courage and caution. It needed both to pursue it steadily from the start, from the moment when, on 12th September, 1938, Göring trumpeted the might of the Luftwaffe to the Nazis assembled at Nuremberg, to the moment when, an

Growing Might. All the power and purposefulness of our air offensive, more formidable every month, is embodied in this Flying Fortress, photographed as it took off for an attack on the " Gneisenau."

hour before dawn on 11th February, 1941, the bright radiance of the landing beam turned for an instant a dark shadow into a shape of ebony and silver, as the first Stirling back from Germany touched down.

The attack on the enemy continues without pause. " We shall bomb Germany by day as well as by night in ever-increasing measure," said the Prime Minister, broadcasting to the world on 22nd June. This is not a threat only, it is a statement of fact. Bomber Command is translating these words into action. Its pilots and crews do not trace

at vast speed fantastic patterns in the sky as did their comrades of Fighter Command when the Battle of Britain was fought and won. They plod steadily on, taking their aircraft through fair weather or foul, night after night and of late by day, to " the abodes of the guilty." Determination and endurance are said to be among the distinguishing qualities of our race. These they possess in full measure. They are of the same breed as the men who each evening notched their dragon prows into the sun's red rim on the first voyage to Labrador, who braced the yards of the " Golden Hind " to

Growing Mastery. The huge form of the four-engined Stirling typifies the increasing weight and momentum with which Bomber Command is striking, day by day, night after night, into the heart of Germany.

round Cape Horn and who stumbled with Scott from the South Pole.

These twentieth-century " gentlemen of the shade, minions of the moon," have accomplished much in twenty-two months of war. Their hearts are high. They have learnt skill and resource flying in aircraft which, when the war began, were the finest of their kind. Now new types of greater power are in their hands, bearing new bombs of a more deadly fashioning. By day they will go out in these new aircraft with their comrades of Fighter Command ever farther into the confines of the foe. By night they will take them " aloft incumbent on the dusky air " to the farthest town and city of Germany. No chosen target can escape them. The Germans are waging war as they have always waged it : without mercy, respite or limit, with no regard to place or person. Perhaps they may regret the consequences. Perhaps they are already doing so. One thing is certain. Bomber Command will allow no pause, no breathing space. Our attack will go on, fierce because it is relentless, deadly because it is sure.